JEWISH VALUES IN JUNGIAN PSYCHOLOGY

Rabbi Levi Meier, Ph.D.

UNIVERSITY
PRESS OF
AMERICA

Lanham • New York • London

Copyright © 1991 by

University Press of America®, Inc.

4720 Boston Way
Lanham, Maryland 20706

3 Henrietta Street
London WC2E 8LU England

The Meaning and soul of "Hear, O Israel"
Copyright © 1991 by Manfred Altman.

Library of Congress Cataloging-in-Publication Data

Meier, Levi.
Jewish values in Jungian Psychology / Levi Meier.
p.   cm.
Includes bibliographical references and indexes.
1. Judaism and psychoanalysis.   2. Judaism and psychology.
3. Jung, C. G. (Carl Gustav), 1875-1971.   I. Title..
BM538.P68M44   1991
296.3'875—dc20   91-4316 CIP

ISBN 0–8191–8323–7 (cloth, alk. paper)
ISBN 0–8191–8324–5 (pbk., alk. paper)

 The paper used in this publication meets the minimum requirements of
American National Standard for Information Sciences—Permanence
of Paper for Printed Library Materials, ANSI Z39.48–1984.

Also by Levi Meier:

Jewish Values in Bioethics (Ed., 1986)

Jewish Values in Psychotherapy (1988)

Jewish Values in Health and Medicine (Ed., 1991)

CONTENTS

Dedication

With Love,
To My Wife, Marcie

In Gratitude To

James Kirsch
(1901-1989)

ACKNOWLEDGEMENTS

I am delighted to express my appreciation and gratitude to my colleagues, friends and family who have critically read portions of this book and offered valuable suggestions. They are: Rabbi Reuven P. Bulka, Rabbi David Ellenson, Gilda Frantz, Thomas Hersh, Mark Levine, Miriam Lippel, Chana Meier, Marcie Meier, Fred Rosner, Zanwil Sperber, J. Marvin Spiegelman, Paula Van Gelder and Kathleen M. Wulf.

I would like to extend special appreciation to Manfred Altman of London, England for his valuable suggestions. Furthermore, he facilitated my incorporating material by his late father, Rabbi Dr. Adolf (Avraham) Altmann, of blessed memory, in Chapter II and as Chapter III of this book. I am honored to present the first English translation of Rabbi Altmann's article on "The Meaning and Soul of 'Hear, O Israel.'"

Cedars-Sinai Medical Center has served as the optimal setting for examining the relationship between Judaism and Jungian psychology. The patients' spiritual and psychological issues have served as a stimulus and catalyst for me to examine and probe the complexity of the human psyche. Cedars-Sinai Medical Center has become my Temple, a unique Temple of Healing.

The Board of Directors, Board of Governors and administration have continuously assisted and encouraged the multifaceted expansion of the Chaplaincy Department. For all of the above, I acknowledge my appreciation and gratitude.

Gita Fuchs Rosenwald deserves recognition for her meticulous and careful production of the final work.

I would like to express my ongoing gratitude to the late Dr. James Kirsch. Our enduring relationship is described in Chapter VII of this work, "Reflections on the Death of my Analyst."

The dedication of this book to my wife, Marcie, is symbolic of my profound love for my partner in life.

Chapter II was published under the title "The Dynamics of Parent-Child Relationship: A Psycho-Judaic Perspective" in the *Journal of Psychology and Judaism*, volume 13, number 2, Summer 1989.

Chapter V was published in an abbreviated version under the title "Heroic and Shameful Behavior: A Psycho-Judaic Perspective" in the *Journal of Psychology and Judaism*, volume 14, number 2, Summer 1990.

Chapter VIII was published in the *New York State Journal of Medicine*, 1991.

PREFACE

In view of Jung's emphasis on the centrality of the religious instinct in the psyche of each individual, it is puzzling to note how scant Jewish scholarship is regarding Jungian psychology. Consequently, Jungian psychologists have underutilized the wealth of Jewish Biblical, Talmudic and Midrashic sources in explaining and amplifying some basic Jungian theories.

This reluctance on the part of the Jewish community to embrace Jungian psychology can be explained in two distinct ways. First, Judaism as a religious tradition has conservative tendencies. For example, Martin Buber's I-Thou philosophy and Viktor Frankl's logotherapy system have only recently been embraced by Jewish writers and thinkers. Secondly, it is difficult for the Jewish community to accept Jung's contribution to Western and Eastern civilization in light of his alleged Nazi links in the early 1930's.

This introductory book serves to build a bridge between Jung's psychology and the Jewish tradition. In Chapter I, Jung's relationship with Sigmund Freud is discussed, as well as their ultimate split. I suggest a new theory regarding the Freud-Jung controversy, relating it to the split between Judaism and Christianity. Jung's involvement with Nazism is also explored. Chapter II offers the first Jewish theory of individuation based on the *sequential* order of the Five Books of Moses. Chapter III, the first English translation of Rabbi Adolf (Avraham) Altmann's article on the *Shema* ("Hear, O Israel") demonstrates how the Jewish declaration of faith requires an ever-deepening inner development throughout life. Chapter IV discusses the centrality of soul consciousness in Judaism and its implications for the interrelationship of analytic psychology and religion. Chapter V describes how Jung's concept of the union of opposites is manifest in the bipolar nature of human beings. Chapter VI illustrates how Jacob's lonely night journey serves as a paradigm for every individual's journey through life. In this chapter, I *imagine* what Jacob's thoughts and feelings were at various stages in his life. Chapter VII presents my personal reflections on the death of my analyst, Dr. James Kirsch, and more significantly, my thoughts on how he exemplified the integration of Judaism and Jungian psychology. Chapter VIII, a review essay on *Freud and Moses*, complements the discussion of the Freud-Jung controversy. It also furthers the theme of individuation by demonstrating Freud's struggle with his Jewish identity.

I hope that this book will illustrate that concepts of Jungian psychology can help one achieve a deeper understanding of Jewish teachings. At the same time, the study of Jewish traditions can enhance and amplify Jung's mode of understanding the human psyche.

PART I

INTRODUCTION

CHAPTER I

JUDAISM AND JUNGIAN PSYCHOLOGY

I.   Introduction

This chapter, entitled "Judaism and Jungian Psychology" -- which also serves as the introduction to *Jewish Values in Jungian Psychology* -- was written after this entire book was near completion. Throughout the process of preparing this book, I encountered some unusual comments which require elaboration and analysis. One Jungian publishing house initially responded enthusiastically when first queried, stating that "this book would be very interesting and marketable, since it would be the *first* such book on Judaism and Jungian psychology by a rabbi/psychologist." Some of my friends who are also clinical psychologists thought that my interest in Jungian psychology was unusual, since Carl Gustav Jung was alleged to have Nazi sympathies. One person even suggested that perhaps my real topic of investigation and exploration ought to be "Judaism and Freudian psychology." Additionally, some of my colleagues who read first drafts of various chapters felt intimidated by the strength of the unconscious as expressed in the following chapters, and they wondered how the powerful force of the unconscious is reconcilable with the daily religious life of an observant and spiritual Jew.

The relationship between Jungian psychology and Judaism appears enigmatic at best. The *Encyclopedia Judaica* does not even have an entry under the name C.G. Jung. The sole mention of Jung is as Sigmund Freud's foremost disciple, who ultimately individuated from his mentor and established his own theory and school (volume 7, p. 162).

In order to unravel these mysteries and to clarify some aspects of the overall theme of "Judaism and Jungian psychology," I explore the centrality of the unconscious in Judaic thought and analyze the split between Freud and Jung and its ongoing implications. I also investigate and describe Jung's initial attitude toward the 1933 National Socialist government of

Germany. Additionally, I speculate as to why the "Jewish" Freud selected the "Christian" Jung as his Joshua, his heir.

The commonality between Judaism and Jungian psychology is the centrality of the unconscious in the development of *each individual.* Indeed, various types of religious experiences are common and accessible to all people (James, 1902). Moses, the primary teacher of the Jewish people, first *experienced* God through the burning bush (Exodus 3:2-4) and subsequently became "the teacher." The religious experience, emanating from the unconscious, was the necessary step in the development of the Jewish religion. The reverse process, of first receiving the Divine law and then experiencing divinity, could logically and psychologically *never* have taken place.

Jung's explanation of the psyche similarly allows for the legitimacy of religious experience for *all people.* That is one of the reasons why many religious people gravitate towards a Jungian approach of understanding the psyche.

A basic assumption in analytical psychology suggests that certain factors in the psyche operate without conscious awareness, yet influence conscious life. This assumption is fundamental to the analysis of the psyche, which undertakes to reach the roots of issues, not only their external manifestations. The existence of the unconscious and of its powerful influence on thought and behavior permeated Biblical and world literature long before its discovery by Freud and Jung. Psychoanalysis and analytical psychology clarified, elucidated and defined the terms of the unconscious and established the general concepts so that these terms could be utilized in an educational and instructive manner.

II.   Sarah's Inner Laughter

One Biblical example of the existence of the unconscious -- and the Bible contains many -- is demonstrated in the description of the announcement of the birth of Isaac (Genesis 18:10-16). Sarah's initial reaction is described as "inner laughter." When God expressed surprise regarding Sarah's laughter, Sarah denied her laughter. A beautiful interpretation of this difficult passage is offered by the *Beit Yisroel*, a twentieth-century Biblical commentary by the Hasidic Rabbi of Gur. He understood that Sarah was unconscious of her laughter, but that "God, who knows all secrets, informed her that in reality she did laugh" (*Beit Yisroel*, Genesis 18:15, p. 40).

In this passage, God expressed concern at Sarah's unconscious laughter. Unconscious laughter eventually impacts on one's conscious reactions. God observes Sarah in totality. In this section, the *Beit Yisroel* refers to God as "He Who knows all secrets." He-Who-Knows-all-secrets is equally concerned with the unconscious as with the conscious. Furthermore, He-Who-Knows-all-secrets desires that each individual also become aware of his or her unconscious. It is a part of each individual, an essential part, and perhaps the pivotal aspect that defines each individual as being created in God's image. The unconscious was discovered in the late nineteenth century but existed since the very beginning of the creation of humanity. Biblical and world literature is filled with descriptions of the awareness and denial of the unconscious.

III.   There Are No Accidents in Jewish Law

Jewish law (*Halakhah*) also recognizes the role of the unconscious by clearly and very prominently differentiating between an intentional (*Mezid*) and an unintentional sin (*Shogeg*). An unintentional sin refers to a prohibited act that is carried out without full awareness. An individual may either state that what was done was legally valid or may claim ignorance of the law. In both cases, the Jewish court does not have the jurisdiction to punish the offender. Other examples of an inadvertent sin include one who commits a crime by accident or by misadventure, without intending the crime, or who commits a crime that, due to unforeseen circumstances, is different from the intended crime.

Although unintentional or inadvertent sins are not punishable by Rabbinic courts, the perpetrator must repent and (in Biblical times) offer a sacrifice, thereby obtaining Divine forgiveness. The offering of a sacrifice is a means of coming closer to God. Indeed, the word *Korban* (sacrifice) is derived from the word *Karav* ("to come close"), implying the need to come closer to God.

What Biblical and Talmudic law is suggesting is that one is partially responsible even for accidental criminal acts. Essentially, the legal system is categorically stating that there are *no accidents*!! Forgetfulness, accidents and inadvertence are part and parcel of everyone's psyche and constitute an integral part of everyone's unconscious. Everyone should express regret, confess and repent, even regarding those acts that were not done consciously. The Talmud is stating very clearly that not all accidents are accidents. Accidents demonstrate a general tendency and inclination of the individual and if this inclination is not noticed, more inadvertent accidents will undoubtedly follow.

This understanding is identical to the concept of the unconscious developed by Jung. Word associations are not accidental; they represent unconscious associations that are not consciously acknowledged. The unconscious is the essential part of each individual that fosters the total development of that person. This includes, but is not limited to, the shadow or dark side of each individual, the anima (feminine) and animus (masculine), the Self and many other parts that are elaborately explained throughout the following chapters.

Another major similarity between Judaism and Jungian psychology is the recognition of the sources of the unconscious. The major sources of the unconscious are dreams, images and visions. Over fifty chapters of the *Torah* (Pentateuch) contain recorded dreams and visions. This essential fact is frequently overlooked, and the unconscious is sometimes not given its full recognition. These sources of the unconscious, which existed in Biblical times, were God's way of communicating with humanity, and these sources still exist for our contemporary society.

Rabbinic literature is aware that the unconscious operates on different levels. Although according to the Talmud (*Yoma* 9b), one form of prophecy ceased during the period of the Second Temple, other forms of Divine communication continued. The Talmud states: "After the death of the latter prophets, Haggai, Zechariah and Malachi,...other forms such as a *Bat Kol* (a heavenly voice) were the ways that God communicated to humanity."

There are numerous statements in Rabbinic literature regarding the status of prophecy after the destruction of the First Temple. R. Johanan's pronouncement, well known among both scholars and laypersons, indicates that prophecy was removed from prophets and given to fools (Talmud, *Bava Batra* 12b). A less known, but equally significant statement by R. Avdimi on that same page of the Talmud is that after the destruction of the First Temple, prophecy was taken from the prophets and given to the Sages (*Bava Batra* 12a).

Furthermore, the Zohar (a Jewish mystical work) states (Genesis 238): "Now prophecy has ended and the *Bat Kol* has ended, and man only uses the dream." What the Zohar is suggesting is that the "royal road" has different paths.

In light of these statements from the Talmud and the Zohar, Rabbinic literature teaches us that there are numerous levels of Divine communication: prophecy; the holy spirit (*Ru'ah ha-Kodesh*); the heavenly voice (*Bat Kol*) and dreams. While these four terms describe four distinct, separate processes, they share an underlying commonality. What we learn from all of this is that the destruction of the Temple was such a spiritual devastation that it affected all aspects of life, yet by no means did all forms of prophecy cease. On the contrary, the statements in Rabbinic literature indicate how much more the present-day individual has to be centered in spirituality in order to allow Divine communication to continue.

IV.   Jung, National Socialism and the Jews

The entire topic of Jung's relationship with the Jewish people has already received extensive treatment by Ernst Harms (1946), Aniela Jaffé (1971) and James Kirsch (1982), and I refer the interested reader to those references. However, I would like to present a summary of their views and to quote the letter written by Gershom Scholem regarding this issue.

One allegation of Jung's Nazi sympathies is based on his acceptance of the Presidency of the General Medical Society for Psychotherapy in 1933. Jung was aware of what potential misunderstandings would arise from his acceptance of the presidency. He wrote:

> A moral conflict arose for me as it would for any decent man in this situation. Should I, as a prudent neutral, withdraw into security this side of the frontier and wash my hands in innocence, or should I -- as I was well aware -- risk my skin and expose myself to the inevitable misunderstandings which no one escapes who, from higher

necessity, has to make a pact with the existing political powers in Germany? (Jung, 1934/1964, pp. 535-536)

What Jung had in mind and what he actually accomplished was to transfer the formal character of the organization from national (Germany) to international. Jung officially amended the statutes of the Society and both legally and in actuality, the society was the International General Medical Society for Psychotherapy. Jung clearly stated his reason for accepting the presidency of this organization. He claimed that a medical doctor helps *all* wounded people, whether or not one agrees with the ideology of the wounded. (The medical community in Israel has also conducted itself in a similar fashion. After the War of Liberation [1948], the Sinai campaign [1956], the Six Day War [1967] and the Yom Kippur War [1973], Israeli hospitals and physicians took special pride in caring for wounded Arab prisoners.)

Furthermore, Jung made special provision to allow German Jewish doctors to maintain individual membership in the International Society, although they were excluded from the German section of the Society. The International Society maintained its neutrality as to politics and creed. In 1939, Jung resigned from the presidency of the organization, since Nazi influence was overbearing. Also, whenever possible, Jung always helped his German-Jewish colleagues.

Some critics of Jung point to the 1933 issue of *Zentralblatt*, published under the aegis of the Society and bearing Jung's name as editor, that contained a special German supplement and declaration by Dr. M.H. Göring, obligating the members of the Society to abide by the Nazi ideology. This supplement, however, was a surprise to Jung when it appeared, although his name was attached to the entire issue as the editor of the 1933 *Zentralblatt* (Jaffé, 1971).

At the same time, however, Jung, as a psychologist, discussed the differences between Jewish and non-Jewish psychology. Furthermore, he discussed as a scientific topic the issue of racial psychology. This hint of Jewish "differentness" at this time in history was one of Jung's grave mistakes.

In 1937, Jung publicly criticized the mass movements in Germany, and as a result of his writings and lectures, his writings were later suppressed in Germany and his name was placed on a blacklist.

Jung himself recognized the error in judgment that he had made regarding National Socialism when it first emerged. His admission of this error was verified by Gershom Scholem. Professor Scholem (Jaffé, 1971) wrote a letter that describes a conversation he had with Rabbi Leo Baeck. I quote it in its entirety.

Jerusalem
7 May 1963

Dear Mrs. Jaffé:

As you are so interested in the story of Baeck and Jung, I will write it down for your benefit and have no objection to being cited by you in this matter.

In the summer of 1947 Leo Baeck was in Jerusalem. I had then just received for the first time an invitation to the Eranos meeting in Ascona, evidently at Jung's suggestion, and I asked Baeck whether I should accept it, as I had heard and read many protests about Jung's behavior in the Nazi period. Baeck said" "You must go, absolutely!" and in the course of our conversation told me the following story. He too had been put off by Jung's reputation resulting from those well-known articles in the years 1933-34, precisely because he knew Jung very well from the Darmstadt meetings of the School of Wisdom and would never have credited him with any Nazi and anti-Semitic sentiments. When, after his release from Theresienstadt, he returned to Switzerland for the time (I think it was 1946), he therefore did not call on Jung in Zurich. But it came to Jung's ears that he was in the city and Jung sent a message begging him to visit him, which he, Baeck, declined because of those happenings. Whereupon Jung came to his hotel and they had an extremely lively talk lasting two hours, during which Baeck reproached him with all the things he had heard. Jung defended himself by an appeal to the special conditions in Germany but at the same time confessed to him: "Well, I slipped up" - probably referring to the Nazis and his expectation that something great might after all emerge. This remark, "I slipped up," which Baeck repeated to me several times, remains vividly in my memory. Baeck said that in this talk they cleared up everything that had come between them and that they parted from one another reconciled again. Because of this explanation of Baeck's I accepted the invitation to Eranos when it came a second time.

Yours sincerely,

G. Scholcm

Furthermore, James Kirsch frequently mentioned to me how Jung was personally helpful to him during the Nazi era. Dr. Kirsch also confided to me the first words Jung said to him upon their first meeting after World War II in 1947. Jung said, "I was wrong and I apologize." This apology referred to the fact that in 1933, Jung did not in any way anticipate that the Nazi movement would lead to the destruction of European Jewry.

Despite the aforementioned explanations, the controversy regarding Jung's attitude continues anew and unabated in each decade. The renewed attacks on Jung's alleged anti-Semitism may ultimately refer to the split that took place between Sigmund Freud, "the Jewish spiritual father figure," and Carl Gustav Jung, "the Christian apostate son." Jung had the opportunity to become Freud's spiritual heir, but he chose to individuate from his mentor. This split between Freud and Jung resembles, on an archetypal level, the split between Moses, the teacher of the Jewish people, and Jesus, the teacher of the Christian people. This split may also shed some new light and interpretation on Freud's last work, published in 1939, entitled *Moses and Monotheism*. (See Chapter VIII)

Freud and Jung's friendship and ultimate separation may be perceived as more than a relationship between two great personalities who enriched each other and the world. It also may represent the Jew and the Christian initially cooperating and ultimately separating from one another, each one continuing on a different path. Freud and Jung may also symbolically represent Judaism and Christianity. As a result, there is a tremendous amount of conscious and unconscious thought emotionally attached to the evaluation of why Jung separated from his mentor, Sigmund Freud. Was the split between these two giants reminiscent of the archetypal father-son relationship which is ultimately transformed into a father-son split? In the eyes of many people, Jung became a traitor when he elected to follow his own creative path instead of becoming the "crown prince." However, the seeds of Jung's separation were already planted in Freud's expressed motivation for selecting Jung as his successor.

V.   Freud's Selection of Jung as His Successor

Psychoanalysis was frequently referred to as a "Jewish science," both by its adherents and by its antagonists. Even as late as 1977, when Anna Freud wrote the inaugural lecture for the Sigmund Freud Chair at the Hebrew University in Jerusalem, she stated that "'Psychoanalysis as a Jewish Science' is a title of honor" (*Midstream*, 1978).

Freud, however, rejected the identification of psychoanalysis as a Jewish science. At the second international congress of psychoanalysts in 1910, the newly formed international association chose Jung as its president. Freud's Viennese followers were puzzled by Freud's support of Jung. Freud explained to his followers that "only Jung's appearance has saved psychoanalysis from becoming a Jewish national concern" (Freud, 1908).

Freud hoped that Jung's professional stature, in addition to his Swiss nationality and Christian religion, would guarantee the psychoanalytic movement a future beyond the Jewish Viennese boundaries.

In the early years of psychoanalysis (1902-1909), Freud's small group of followers consisted exclusively of Jews. But none of them impressed him as a plausible successor. Jung, however, would unlock the doors to the outside world.   Freud desired that psychoanalysis achieve general acceptance. Freud was genuinely fond of Jung for some years, but the facts that the Swiss Jung was not Jewish and not from Vienna were pivotal in Freud's decision-making process. Even when Freud's relationship with Jung was going sour, Freud continued to insist that psychoanalysis was not and should not be perceived as a Jewish science.

In 1910, Freud referred to Jung as his "dear son" and said: "I leave you more to conquer than I could manage myself, all of psychiatry and the approval of the civilized world, which is accustomed to regard me as a savage!" (*The Freud/Jung Letters*, 1974, p. 300).

Freud's insistence that psychoanalysis not be perceived as a Jewish science and his selection of Jung as his successor were Freud's ways of obtaining general acceptance and realizing his hope that psychoanalysis would become a universal science.

Interestingly, this thought finds its parallel in Maimonides' explanation of Christianity's and Islam's relationship to Judaism (*Mishneh Torah, Hilkhot Melakhim* 11:4, uncensored edition).

Maimonides sees both Christianity and Islam as positive historical influences -- to prepare the *world* for monotheism. By spreading knowledge of the Bible and the idea of the commandments, the seeds are planted that will reach full fruition at some future eschatological date. Christianity and Islam have been assigned significant roles in the Divine historical design.

Maimonides states:

But it is beyond the human mind to fathom the designs of the Creator; for our ways are not His ways, neither are our thoughts His thoughts. All these matters relating to Jesus of Nazareth and the Ishmaelite (Mohammed) who came after him only served to clear the way for King Messiah, to prepare the whole world to worship God with one accord...

Furthermore, Maimonides suggests that Christianity and Islam will also reach the four corners of the world. He states:

...Thus, the Messianic hope, the Torah, and the commandments have become familiar topics -- topics of conversation (among the inhabitants) of the far isles and many people...

Maimonides retrospectively and Freud prospectively felt and saw the need to broaden their beliefs and philosophies in order to achieve general acceptance. For Judaism as a whole, including the very fundamental Messianic hope of universal belief in monotheism, Christianity and Islam became necessary to achieve the eschatological hope of worshipping God in full accord with all people of the world. For psychoanalysis, Freud also saw the need for wider acceptance than the Viennese Jewish circle of Freud's followers. Christianity and Islam were to Judaism what Jung was to Freud.

VI.   Jung Rejects His Father Figure

It appears that Jung's rejection of some of Freud's theories is based not only on theoretical and clinical differences, but also on Jung's refusal to accept Freud's psychoanalytical theory, which was presented with the potency of religious dogma.

Jung felt that Freud was emotionally involved in his sexual theory to an extraordinary degree. Jung recalled how, in 1910, Freud said to him,

> My dear Jung, promise me never to abandon the sexual theory. That is the most essential thing of all. You see, we must make a dogma of it, an unshakable bulwark. (Jung, 1965, p. 150)

Jung understood that a dogma represented an indisputable confession of faith, whose aim is to suppress doubts. He knew that he would never be able to accept such an attitude.

In 1909, Freud and Jung traveled together to a lecture tour in the United States. During that ship voyage, they each analyzed the other's dreams. As a result of this intimacy, their whole relationship deteriorated. Jung reports (Jung, 1965, p. 158):

> Freud had a dream -- I interpreted it as best I could, but added that a great deal more could be said about it if he would supply me with some additional details from his private life. Freud's response to these words was a curious look -- a look of the utmost suspicion. Then he said, "But I cannot risk my authority!" At that point he lost it altogether. That sentence burned itself into my memory; and in it the end of our relationship was already foreshadowed. Freud was placing personal authority above truth.

Once again Jung experienced Freud's theory of psychoanalysis as taking the form of religious authority and dogma.

Furthermore, Jung was never able to agree with Freud's concept that a dream is a "facade," behind which its meaning lies hidden. For Jung, the unconscious and dreams, which are its direct manifestations, are natural processes. There is no latent or hidden dream in Jungian theory. The dream is a *symbolic* representation of the state of the *psyche*, showing the contents of the personal psyche in personified form as persons, objects and situations that reflect the patterning of the mind. Jung criticized Freud's theory for overlooking the fact that many dreams seem to mean exactly what they say. For Jung, dreams were a self-representation of the state of the psyche, presented in symbolic form. The purpose of dreams is to compensate for the one-sided distortions of the waking ego; they are therefore in the service of the individuation process, helping the waking "self" to face itself more objectively and consciously.

Jung's understanding that a dream is what it appears to be finds its parallel in the Talmud. Interestingly, Jung quotes the Talmud: "The dream is its own interpretation" (Jung, *Psychology and Religion*, p. 31). Jung explains that there is no reason to assume that a dream would lead us astray. The exact quote that Jung was referring to is found in the Talmud (*Berakhot* 55b): "*Kol ha-Halomot holhin ahar ha-Peh*." This means that all dreams depend upon the dreamer's associations and circumstances. Both Jung and the Talmud seemingly concur that a dream is not a facade, but rather a symbolic representation of the state of the dreamer's psyche.

Although Freud initially wanted Jung to be his heir, Jung individuated from his mentor. Freudians see Jung in classical Oedipal terms, desiring to supplant the father. Freud even remarked that Jung harbored a death-wish against him (Jung, 1965, p. 156). This process of individuation has taken on additional symbolic meaning. Jung, the potential crown prince to Freud, refused to become the Joshua of the psychoanalytic movement. Who did Jung become symbolically? Jung's relationship with his biological father, a Protestant minister, had also deteriorated. For the young Jung saw his father holding fast to the theological traditions that he served, but somehow C.G. Jung's experiences and visions led him to believe that his father was not fulfilling the will of a living God. From Jung's perspective, his father's bondage to tradition and dogma caused fits of depression that led to the deterioration of his father's health, and eventually to his death.

One of Jung's early visions reflected God's unhappiness with the Church and the Christian tradition. He shared his vision by stating:

> I saw before me the cathedral, the blue sky. God sits on His golden throne, high above the world -- and from under the throne an

enormous turd falls upon the sparkling new roof, shatters it, and breaks the walls of the cathedral asunder. (Jung, 1965, p. 39)

The deep meaning of this vision was expressed as "God himself had disavowed theology and the Church founded upon it" (Jung, 1965, p. 93).

The image that eventually emerges from Jung's recollection of his relationship with his father is that established theology blocks the way to God, and therefore the direct relationship of father and son is also disrupted.

Jung states:

My memory of my father is of a sufferer stricken with an Amfortas wound, a "fisher king" whose wound would not heal -- that Christian suffering for which the alchemists sought the panacea. I as a "dumb" Parsifal was the witness of this sickness during the years of my boyhood, and, like Parsifal, speech failed me. (Jung, 1965, p. 215)

Jung departed from Freud and was disenchanted by his own father's tradition. Who was Jung going to follow?

VII.   Freud and Moses, Jung and ?

Throughout Freud's life, the image of Moses was foremost in his mind. Freud closely identified with Moses. Moses, the leader of the Jewish people, who also saw himself as the ultimate leader and teacher for all people, served as a supreme archetype figure for Freud. In 1897, Freud dreamt that "someone led me to the top of a hill and showed me Rome half-shrouded in mist;...the theme of 'the promised land seen from afar' was obvious in it" (Freud, *Standard edition*, The Interpretation of Dreams). In 1901, on his first visit to Rome, he was fascinated with Michelangelo's Moses. He identified with this superhuman figure in terms of his own mission as well.

In 1909, Freud wrote to Jung:

We are certainly getting ahead. If I am Moses, then you are Joshua and will take possession of the promised land of psychiatry, which

I shall only be able to glimpse from afar. *(The Freud/Jung Letters,* 1974, pp. 196-197)

It has even been suggested (Hogenson, 1983) that Freud's authority showed characteristics of an attempt to found a religion in which he would be the principal prophet and lawgiver. For Freud, the authority of the traditional religious God had passed, with the succession of authority given to the unconscious. Freud's new science of psychoanalysis would now legislate for all of humanity.

This development explains why Freud wrote to his Swiss friend, Oskar Pfister: "Quite by the way, why did none of the devout create psychoanalysis? Why did one have to wait for a completely godless Jew?" *(Freud-Pfister,* 1963, p. 64).

Jung's contrary view of the psyche is not a simple empirical deviation, but rather suggests a heresy. Jung is transformed into an apostate. Jung does not legislate how the unconscious should be interpreted. He suggests that each person *participate* in the fundamental reality of the unconscious.

By contrast, Freud's obsession with the lawgiver, Moses, was lifelong and culminated in his controversial book, *Moses and Monotheism.*

VIII. Freud's *Moses and Monotheism*

Moses and Monotheism was Freud's last published work before he died in 1939. The book is a very difficult work to understand. Its relevance for this chapter is that Freud de-Judaized Moses, transformed him into an Egyptian and then claimed that the Jews had murdered him.

Although the Hebrew name *Moshe* is indeed a translation from the Egyptian name *Monius* (Ibn Ezra, Exodus 2:10), the Biblical text and all traditional scholars clearly understand Moses to be a Hebrew and not an Egyptian (Exodus 2:1).

I would like to suggest a few hypotheses in order to try to understand Freud's bold and contrary thesis. His book may be seen as a product of the 1930's and the rising anti-Semitism by "proving" to the world that the Jews are not God's "chosen people" but are rather the "chosen people" of Moses, the Egyptian (Bakan, 1958).

Alternately, one may suggest that Freud's obsession with the image of Moses motivated Freud to destroy Moses and have himself resurrected as the real Moses to his people.

It may also be suggested that Freud wanted to de-Judaize himself and stress his independence from the Jewish heritage so that psychoanalysis would ultimately be perceived as a world science and not a "Jewish science."

Perhaps, near the end of his life, Freud searched for a way to reach the world at large. He created a new Moses, who would possibly serve as a link to both the Jewish and the non-Jewish world.

IX. The Unconscious (a Dream) Amplifies the Archetypal Conflict between Freud and Jung

Freud's identification with Moses and his desire that the Swiss Christian, Jung, become his Joshua had not been fulfilled. Who did Jung symbolically become?

While all these thoughts were brewing in my mind, on November 30, 1988, I had the following dream that may shed some light on the question of who Jung symbolically represented.

Sitting at a round table are Freud, Marx, Adler, Einstein and Jesus. Each person has a children's book describing himself and his teachings. I announce that these forthcoming children's books are not for everyone.

When I awoke, I did not understand why Jung was omitted and Jesus included. Furthermore, I questioned the presence of Freud, Marx, Adler and Einstein -- who all lived in the 19th and 20th centuries -- alongside Jesus, who lived 19 centuries ago. And why was I included amongst this group at this time in my life? What would be the advantage of having children's books on all of these people's teachings? And why are these books not for everyone?

Interpretation:

This dream sheds light on many different questions, with its symbolism of the children's books and the round table, and the symbolic meaning of each individual selected to appear. However, the aspect of the dream that relates to this topic of Judaism and Jungian psychology is the substitution of Jesus for Jung. Jesus and Jung both individuated from their spiritual heritage. Jesus departed from Moses, and Jung departed from Freud. Jung's departure from Freud has been perceived as a departure from Moses, due to Freud's identification with Moses. Freud wanted Jung to become his Joshua. When Jung decided not to become Joshua, he was labeled as someone who deserted his spiritual father.

The renewed debates on Jung's alleged Nazi sympathies are, in reality, partially intertwined with his departure from his Moses, Freud. These discussions are further linked to Jung's emphasis on the racial differentness of the Jewish people, particularly since he wrote these theories during the 1930's -- a time of rising anti-Semitism in Germany and Europe.

Jung was severely limited in his comprehension of anti-Semitism as an essential current in Christian European culture. However, once the reality of anti-Semitism became evident to Jung, he turned away from it as decisively as he could. By 1936, Jung had lectured and written about his misgivings regarding the events in Germany and referred to "German psychology," just as he had much earlier referred to "Jewish psychology."

Unconsciously, many Jewish people, and non-Jews as well, lump Jung together with Jesus as two who departed from the archetype Moses.

Jung's departure, however, does not represent a betrayal of the unconscious but on the contrary, it reflects the process of individuation based on the unconscious.

X.   The Unconscious and Daily Religious Life

Another issue in the relationship between Jungian psychology and Judaism is the impact that the unconscious has on daily religious rituals. Jung's view of the process of individuation based on the unconscious can enhance the individual's connection to God, while also enhancing daily religious life.

Moses's experience of the burning bush was always with him, as is every numinous experience of every individual. The daily religious life represents a connection to the collective communities, the family, the Jewish people and humanity. While this connection is maintained, the individual's connection continues as well. Sometimes more emphasis is placed on the collective and sometimes more is placed on the individual. This process ultimately reflects a balancing process, whereby different needs are fulfilled and different inner and outer events are experienced.

Both individually and collectively, the unconscious can become the quintessential aspect of daily religious life and life in general. This balancing process allows one to move in the direction of individuation and self-actualization.

XI.   The Process of Individuation

This process of individuation, which is defined and expanded in the next few chapters, represents a direction rather than a goal to achieve. The person is in a constant state of movement, stability, movement and stability, whereby ultimately, movement represents a new kind of stability.

When family members exclaim to a relative, "How much you have changed!," an appropriate response could be, "Thank you for sharing your observation with me," rather than becoming defensive regarding noticeable changes. The question of "Who am I?" is constantly open to new images and changes.

This process is lifelong, and it represents the beautiful journey of *everyone's* life. The relationship between Judaism and Jungian psychology is manifest in the journey of everyone's life, collective and individual. The rest of this book describes some aspects of this process.

References

Bakan, D. (1958). *Sigmund Freud and the Jewish mystical tradition.* Princeton, N.J.: Van Nostrand.

Beit Yisroel. (No date). Yisroel ben Avraham Mordechai MeGur. Jerusalem: Hed Press.

Encyclopedia Judaica. (16 vols.) (1972). Jerusalem: Keter Publishing House.

Freud, S. (1963). *Psycho-analysis and faith: The letters of Sigmund Freud and Oskar Pfister.* Edited by H. Meng and E.L. Freud. Trans. by E. Mosbacher. London: Hogarth Press.

Freud, S. (24 vols.) (1953-64). *The standard edition of the complete psychological works of Sigmund Freud.* London: Hogarth Press.

The Freud/Jung letters: The correspondence between Sigmund Freud and C.G. Jung. (1974). Edited by William McGuire. Trans. by R. Manheim and R.F.C. Hull. Princeton, N.J.: Princeton University Press (Bollingen Series).

Harms, E. (1946). C.G. Jung -- Defender of Freud and the Jews. *Psychiatric Quarterly, 30.*

Hogenson, G.B. (1983). *Jung's struggle with Freud.* Notre Dame: University of Notre Dame Press.

The Holy Scriptures. (2 vols.) (1917). Philadelphia: Jewish Publication Society.

Jaffé, A. (1971). *Jung's last years and other essays.* Trans. by R.F.C. Hull and Murray Stein. Dallas: Spring Publications, Inc.

James, W. (1902). *The varieties of religious experience.* Garden City, N.Y.: Dolphin Books.

Jung, C.G. (20 vols.) (1969). *Collected works*. Princeton, N.J.: Princeton University Press.

Jung, C.G. (1965). *Memories, dreams, reflections*. Rev. ed. Edited by A. Jaffé. Trans. by R. and C. Winston. New York: Vintage Books.

Jung, C.G. (1934/1964). A rejoinder to Dr. Bally. In *The collected works of C.G. Jung* (vol. 10). Princeton: Princeton University Press, 1964. (Originally published, 1934.)

Jung, C.G. (Ed.) (1933). Zentralblatt fur Psychotherapie und ihre Grenzgebiete. Leipzig, Germany.

Kirsch, J. (1982). Carl Gustav Jung and the Jews: The real story. *Journal of Psychology and Judaism. 6(2)*. Spring/Summer.

Maimonides, M. (12th century) (1962). *Mishneh Torah*. (6 vols.). New York: M.P. Press.

Midstream. (1978). *XXIV, 32*. March.

The Talmud (18 vols.) (1961). I. Epstein (Ed.). London: Soncino Press.

The Zohar. (5 vols.) (1931-34). Trans. by H. Sperling, M. Simon and P.P. Levertoff. London: Soncino Press.

PART II

THE PROCESS OF INDIVIDUATION

CHAPTER II

INDIVIDUATION AND *SHEMA YISROEL* (HEAR, O ISRAEL)

A healthy parent-child relationship will foster and promote the process of individuation. Individuation is a technical psychological word which describes how people utilize their genetic and environmental resources, including consciousness and unconsciousness, to best develop the emergence of a "re-newed" and creative individual.

The process of individuation begins from the moment of birth and terminates at death. It represents a constant and dynamic fluidity of movement, reevaluation and reappraisal of where one has been, where one is and where one is going. The only constant in life is change. This change manifests itself through continuous attachment to and detachment from people, thoughts and objects. Members of one's family, friends and associates assume different significance throughout life. The dominance of attachments may start with a parent, refocus on siblings, friends, and professional colleagues, and ultimately be directed to one's spouse and oneself.

In addition to the parent-child relationship, other aspects of lifelong development are also essential to the process of individuation. These include shadow, anima-animus, old wise man, *mana*-personality, Self, magician, Great Mother and others (Jung, 1970, vol. 7, pp. 173-241.).

Underlying all of these relationships is an ongoing development of oneself, which ultimately is reflected in the choices that one makes. This changing attachment to people finds its parallel in the areas of the development of thought and in relationship to attachment to objects. As the psychological life cycle developmental process unfolds, liberalism frequently is transformed into conservatism, logical dictates of the mind make space for experimental and mystical modalities, and micro issues assume less significance than universal macro issues of life and death. Objects and symbols also take on varying shades of meaning throughout life.   In childhood and adolescence, playful objects and idealized fantasies are paramount; in young adulthood and maturity, objects which represent personal and professional security and advancement are accrued; and in senescence, objects that signify a never-ending present become more significant.

All of these changes represent a normal psychological process. The only "absolute" truth regarding attachment to and detachment from people, thoughts and objects is that the "truth" constantly changes throughout one's life.   Thus the picture which emerges is a necessary recognition of a changing self, on a conscious and unconscious level, at different phases of life.

This process of individuation helps to maintain physical, emotional and spiritual health. Individuality allows for the process of centering, a deep understanding of self and a union with God. Indeed, a hypothesis of the genesis of cancer is that the abnormality of the human cell is a mirror image of the pathology of the human soul. Individuation represents a homeostatic equilibrium of the biological, psychological, sociological and spiritual dimensions of the individual. If this process is thwarted or stagnates, the system itself overcompensates for this deficiency by presenting some pathology. Illness is life's natural process of healing.

The mirror image and relationship of the physical and spiritual dimensions are indicated in many religions, cultures and philosophical systems by the use of the same root word for breath and for soul or spirit. The following table (Meany, 1988, p. 203) demonstrates this concept:

LANGUAGE	TERM	MEANINGS
Greek	psyche	breath; soul
	pneuma	breath; air; spirit
Latin	anima	breath; soul
	spiritus	breath; spirit
Hebrew	nefesh	one that breathes; life; soul
	ru'ah	breath; wind; spirit
Arabic	nafs	breath; soul
	ruh	breath; wind; spirit

LANGUAGE	TERM	MEANINGS
Chinese	ch'i	breath; air; spirit
Japanese	ki	air; spirit; soul; heart

Bio-psycho-social-spiritual interrelatedness is frequently initiated by a centering exercise of breathing. Breathing represents the quintessential criterion of the vitality of life. Homiletically, it can be suggested that the first word of the Bible specifically begins with the symbol *Bet*, a letter which requires a breath, rather than an *Aleph*, the first letter of the Hebrew alphabet, which is silent. Only through a *sound*, only through some movement, can creativity take place. This movement may upset a previously established paradigm, but it also represents growth, development and change.

A similar understanding of the vitality of movement is suggested regarding the formality and the systemization of Jewish law, known as *Halakhah*. The word *Halakhah* is the noun form of the verb meaning "to go" or "to walk." Each step a person takes requires the lifting of one foot, and for that transient time before stability is reestablished, one is in a state of temporary instability -- held in abeyance with one foot on the ground and one foot in the air. Being unstable gives one the opportunity to fill that momentary void with a higher state of being. Thus, each step is a step of elevation and of ascendancy to higher stability.

Both Jewish and Greek philosophers have proclaimed that the world was created through the spoken word. The Mishnah (*Avot* 5:1) states that the world was created through God's ten utterances of "And He said." The Hellenistic tradition likewise put emphasis on *logos*, the word as the vehicle for creation.

The *Bet* of the first word of the Bible, the ten utterances of the creation story, and the *logos* in Greek philosophy, all accentuate the necessity of sound and breathing to herald creativity, dynamism, change and adaptation. The first sound of any day is the rooster crowing "cock-a-doodle-do." This sound signals a new cycle of life, another day of opportunity and a call to the rest of humanity to rise to the occasion.

The process of individuation is similar to the processes of creativity, change and responding to life's new situations. It requires an initial act of centering, with the focus on breathing. As previously indicated, the concept and word for breath and soul can frequently be found in the same or similar etymological roots. Only through the vitality of life can the soul be developed to its fullest. This development allows for a feeling of Divine inspiration and a real union with God. Prophetic images reappear and capture the individual.

Upon completing the donning of phylacteries, one recites two verses from the Prophet Hosea (2:21-2):

> I will *betroth* you to myself forever,

> I will *betroth* you to myself in righteousness, and in justice, in kindness and in mercy.

> I will *betroth* you to myself in faithfulness; and you shall know the Lord.

The phylacteries are a symbolic manifestation of a spiritual engagement ring representing union of the individual with Divine love. The spiritual engagement ring highlights the eternity of the relationship, the experiential aspect of the relationship and the Abrahamic trustfulness of the relationship (Genesis 22:12).

The antithesis of the aforementioned theory of individuation and life vitality is satisfaction with the status quo, complacency and stagnation with certainty of an absolute truth. This stagnation is holding on to a paradigmatic view which is unchanging. In the history of science, new discoveries were frequently shunned because of the disturbing effects on the established theory of paradigm (Kuhn, 1970, pp. 43-52).

Thus, every new theory creates a scientific revolution whereby everything else has to adapt to the new hypothesis. The same circumstance surrounds a psychological view of life. A deeper understanding of oneself is bound to cause changes. The force of psychological theory, known as depth psychology, encourages every individual to probe deeper and deeper within his or her self, so that the Socratic maxim of "know thyself" and the

Shakespearean maxim, "Above all else, to thine own self be true," see their fruition. This approach allows life to be lived to its fullest.

To live life to its fullest requires change in the midst of order and order in the midst of change. This alternating change/order cycle incorporates the attachment/detachment relationship to people, theories, weltanschauung and objects. Throughout the life cycle, not only do attachment and detachment occur, but even within an attachment or detachment phase, the intensity, frequency and duration vary considerably. It is precisely this varying degree of intensity, frequency and duration that represents the rhythmic cycle which allows for individuation.

A central issue in the 2 x 3 factorial design, pictured here,

	people	theory	object
attachment			
detachment			

is the understanding of what is the underlying motivation for change. External changes represent internal psychodynamic changes. When parents' relationships with an adult child become more or less intense, this usually represents a mirror image of the parents' need for a greater or lesser affirmation of love, caring and approval for themselves. This relationship exemplifies one of the most significant principles of psychoanalytic theory, called projection. Projection understands all transferences as manifestations of an internal psychodynamic need. Compliments or criticism primarily reflect upon the evaluator rather than the person who is being evaluated.

What are the necessary psychological processes of emotional individuation in order to become a mature adult? One of the components of this process is the ability to internalize authority: maternal authority, paternal authority, sibling authority, spousal authority and even Divine authority.

The internalization of authority is necessary in order to achieve individuation. This psychological process of internalization has a parallel in one of the most basic areas of physiology -- feeding or eating. A baby is born with a natural reflex of sucking, a process that gives pleasure to both baby and nursing mother. Indeed, this mutual process has also been referred to as the third type of orgasm. As the baby matures, the baby learns to develop mastery and control regarding food intake.

The Midrash implies that inner conflict is sometimes determined by projected external considerations. The classic example relates to the Biblical episode of Joseph's sexual temptation by Potiphar's wife. The Midrash states:

> And Joseph came into the house to do his work. Rab and Samuel differ in their interpretation. Rab said he came to do actual work. Samuel said he came to fulfill his desire with her. However, at that moment, the image of his father appeared to him in the window and said to him: "Joseph! Your brothers' names are destined to be inscribed on the stones of the priestly breastplate and your name among them. Is it your wish that your name be wiped out from among them, and that you be called an associate of harlots?" (Genesis Rabbah, 39:11)

Although Joseph's inner conflict resulted in moral triumph, the psychological process was determined by a projected image of his father and brothers. The Midrash allowed us a glimpse into Joseph's internal psychodynamic process of individuation. Joseph still required the external authority image of his father and brothers.

Psychoanalytic Thoughts and Individuation

Psychoanalytic thought has also amplified the *Eros* or life wish. This wish is a symbolic representation of the affirmation of one's life. It is a method of liberation from the image of one's father and mother. It is the desire to be set free. William Blake poetically stated: "No bird soars too high, if he soars with his own wings" (Blake, 1966).

Individuals may imagine anything at will, as long as they remain true to their own reality. This reality acquires meaning and form for the individual in the course of the process of individuation. Individuation is the consciously-directed journey into self, into the gradual understanding of one's own essence at its highest level of functioning. One's reality, seen this way, is subjective. One becomes aware that whatever one experiences is affected by the self, and that there is a subtle difference between one's own experiences and those of anyone else.

This journey into Self requires a confrontation with one's darkest shadow, a unique suffering of the soul. Jung observed in *Mysterium Conjuntionis*:

> only one who has risked the fight with the dragon and is not overcome by it wins the hoard, the "treasure hard to attain." He alone has a genuine claim to self confidence, for he has faced the dark ground of his self and thereby has gained himself. (Jung, 1970, vol. 14, par. 756)

This unique process is a person's destiny. There is a Yiddish colloquial term that states the same -- the word *Bashert*, which means fated or destined. It is usually used when a couple is engaged: the prospective spouse is called the *Basherte*. This expression is based on the Talmudic statement (*Sotah* 2a):

> Forty days prior to birth, a heavenly voice proclaims the daughter of so-and-so is destined to marry so-and-so.

This means that each person's spouse is specifically divinely selected to be in this relationship. It is precisely the compatibility and the incompatibility aspects of the marital relationship that constellate in the other the necessary process of individuation.

This process is lifelong. The ability to be aware of parental or other authority figures is found in the psyche. What is the psyche and what is the reaction to a parent complex?

The parent complex can be all-encompassing: the way we feel about our bodily life, the basic fears and guilts, how we behave in closeness, intimacy, and sexuality, how we feel when we are ill, and our patterns of relating to family and friends. The parent complex is not our parents'; it is our complex. It is the way in which our psyche has taken up our parents. Parents pass on fears and uncertainties to their children. The difficulty lies not only in the expression of these feelings, but in the impenetrable loyalty to what has been expressed. This parent complex protects one from experiencing life, and it encapsulates one from feeling and thinking what one feels and thinks.

A gap is created between us and life. Life passes by and the richness of life is ignored. We go through life in a state of psychological paralysis. This paralysis frequently determines whether we are happy or sad. The parent within us so long ruled the stereotypes of feelings and values that we lack awareness of our own value as individuals. This pattern may even continue long after a parent's death.

Erich Fromm (1950) amplified Freud's theory that the Oedipus complex is the core of every neurosis. Freud's assumption is that the child is bound to the parent of the opposite sex and that mental illness results if the child remains fixated at that stage of development. Fromm translated Freud's discovery from the area of sex into that of interpersonal relations. The essence of psychological incest is the child's lifelong desire to remain attached to those early protecting and influential parent figures. The act of birth is only one step in the direction of freedom and independence. To cut the navel string, not in the physical but in the psychological sense, is the greatest challenge to human development. A person can be an adult and yet be a psychological fetus. He or she fails to become a full human being and remains dependent. This incestuously-oriented person is capable of feeling intimate only to those with whom he or she is familiar. In this orientation, all feelings and ideas are judged not in terms of good and evil or true and false, but of familiar and unfamiliar. Ultimately, everyone must break the incestuous ties and become psychologically free in order to become human.

This process of individuation or of humanization takes place not only in terms of parental authority, but also with other forms of the collective, such as the nation, race, state, social class and political parties. The humanization of mankind is the development from protective incest to freedom. Love for a spouse is dependent on overcoming incestuous strivings. The Bible states (Genesis 2:24): "Therefore shall a man leave his father and mother and shall cleave unto his wife." When this process takes place, life can be lived to its fullest.

This freedom to individuate is sometimes stifled in religious institutions. Institutional religions have lost the living image of the Divine

Presence. The Bible states (Exodus 25:8): "You shall make for me a Tabernacle and I shall dwell in *your* midst." Scripture emphasizes in *your* midst, not in the edifice or structure which you build. A synagogue is constructed to facilitate the process of encountering the image of a living God. A synagogue is a symbol which requires active participation in raising the consciousness of the living God. Jung states:

> A symbol really lives only when it is the best and highest possible expression of something divined, but not yet known, even to the observer. For under these circumstances it provokes participation. It advances and creates life. (Jung, 1970, *Psychological Types*, vol. 6, p. 605)

The idea of the ever-enlarging meaning of a symbol can only take place when individuals are able to take a leap into the unknown. The concept of a Tabernacle or synagogue as a beautiful symbol for the living Divine Presence can only be meaningful if individuals can imbue the symbol with creative meaning.

The emancipation from an edifice and the recreation of symbols are the basis of true development. Emancipation has been the central motif of the historical origins of the Jewish people. Abraham is told to leave his country and become a wanderer. Moses is brought up as a stranger in an unfamiliar environment, away from his family and even from his own people. This period of isolation is necessary to create the freedom to fight against an incestuous worship of the soil, of idols and of the state.

It is the great tragedy of Judaism, and other religions as well, that the very principles of freedom that represent their quintessential reason for existence have become perverted. The Mishnah (*Avot* 6:2) states: "Do not read *Charut* (engraved) but *Cherut* (freedom), for you cannot have a truly free individual except for one who engages in the study of Torah." The study of Torah is the primary basis of life in order to achieve freedom. Organizations that are governed by religious bureaucracy worship the means, the commandments, the edifices rather than experiencing the rituals as a way to worship God.

In many ways, organized religion has stifled religious development. The image of a living God has died in the pathology of religious bureaucracy.

In my clinical practice, I have observed that a substantial number of cases fall into two categories: (a) young adults who find it exceedingly difficult to individuate; and (b) parents who have no *Nachat* (pride) from their children because their children have not lived up to their wishes. In these two categories, both the young adults and the parents have not individuated. The young adults feel completely conflicted and guilt-ridden about their process of humanization and the parents frequently live their own lives vicariously through their children.

In both situations there is no relationship to a transpersonal self. Frequently such people live their whole lives based on principles, rules and regulations. If one tries to live by ideals, one experiences a sense of unreality. There are "musts," "ought to's," "should's," and "have to's," but somehow the person gets lost in the shuffle. The connection between the ego and self is non-existent. The ego is too frightened to receive from the unconscious. There is a genuine fear of life. The spirit is "analyzed," dreams are ignored and feelings of ecstasy are read, but not sung. Even Biblical poetry and images are intentionally avoided. The sky and clouds become scientific concepts rather than expressions of the majesty and natural revelation of God. God's revelation becomes confined to Abraham and Moses and is concretized into laws and norms. People block their unconscious, ignore their dreams, stifle their inner spiritual journey, and their soul dies. They commit not suicide, not homicide, not fratricide, not genocide, but Deicide. They ignore their Divine soul.

Why do some people conduct themselves in such a way? These people sacrifice their unique destiny and adjust to the form of the vast majority of people in our culture. The "adjusted" person is protected only from manifest conflicts. This seemingly adjusted person may develop the accepted avenues of illness with which our society is stricken. From obesity to anorexia, from cardiovascular ailments to cancer and alcoholism, all these and others are the accepted maladies our culture offers in place of the potentially frightening experience of being alone with oneself and the implanted Divine image of God. This understanding will enable individuals to assume greater responsibility in relating their psyche, soul and attitudes to bodily health.

"You shall love your neighbor as yourself" (Leviticus 19:18) is perhaps the best known and yet least understood statement of the Bible. The ability to "love" your neighbor means having the capacity to experience concern, responsibility, respect and understanding of another person. The desire for that other person's growth is rooted in the experience of being able to accept and to love oneself to the utmost. To be able to sense the Divine aspect within oneself enables one to see the Divine in one's neighbor, regardless of his or her impoverished state. Whether one's neighbor is elderly and senile or young and psychotic, each person still carries that vital force of Divine life.

The importance of the process of individuation is not the end result but the process itself. This process is the systematic confrontation of the ego with the contents of the unconscious. The unconscious is God's forgotten language or God's way of guiding each individual. The experience of this process is one's experience of *Shekhinah*, God's Divine Presence. This is the interpretation of the Scriptural description of man as created in the image of God (Genesis 1:27), that something Divine is contained in the soul. Religion must refocus from its traditional emphasis on dogma and theology to a dialogue with an immanent God. This focus establishes a constant dynamic between the ego and the transpersonal self.

Rabbi Akiba stated that the commandment of loving one's neighbor as oneself is the key and central principle of the Torah (Jerusalem Talmud, *Nedarim* 89:4). This humanistic statement is also connected to the last two words of the sentence which read "For I am God" (Leviticus, 19:18). The humanistic statement is transformed into a theistic-humanistic one. Thus, I suggest that Rabbi Akiba is indicating that the centrality of the Torah is the present, the here-and-now imbued with the Divine spirit in the eyes and ears of the beholder. Indeed, all else is commentary!!

The Parent-Child Relationship and Individuation

Having delineated the process of individuation, I would like to suggest the interrelatedness between the process of individuation and the parent-child relationship.

Religious beliefs, practices, values and experiences are deeply intertwined in the core of a person's psychological personality (Spero, 1985). This relationship is usually denied by most people. Some patients view their personality and religious life as completely dichotomous from one another. A few examples indicate the contrary. A pathological religious behavior is usually a manifestation of an unusual psychological need. An obsessive-compulsive personality is always indicated in an overly scrupulous attention to minute details, to such an extent that the underlying essence and principle is frequently overlooked. A woman with a repressed sexual personality may, unknowingly, intentionally elongate the normal time period of sexual abstinence. A depressed or angry personality may conduct religious life in a similar modality some of the time. Thus a "disordered religiosity is an expression of disordered psychological need" (Spero, 1985, p.11).

Another illustration of personality's impact on religious life is the observation that the identical religious act or belief performed by two individuals may reflect on the two people differently. In one, it may produce a conflict of the psyche; in the other, an intense religious experience. Thus, the core personality is completely enmeshed in one's religious life.

Some people may even distort religious belief in order to allow it to be reconciled with their other belief systems. An example that has recently been accentuated is the manner in which some Rabbinic and observant lay people sometimes derogatively refer to non-Jews, when the Bible expressly states that all of humanity was created in the image of God.

Regarding the parent-child relationship and one's relationship to God and the image of God, the human object relationship influences the Divine object relationship and vice versa (Guntrip, 1969). A person's attitude toward reward and punishment, repentance, prayer and blessing frequently correlates with that person's attitudes toward God and parents...and even transference to a therapist. The Bible states that we are the children of God (Deuteronomy 14:1). Thus, God is like a parent figure.

The process of individuation from one's home of origin, birthplace and land, which Abraham experienced (Meier, 1988), is the guide for each of us. By leaving our parents psychologically, as well as in other ways, we are then able to experience our parents, parental figures, and God as an I-thou religious, spiritual encounter leading to the possibility of numinous experiences.

This process of individuation allows us to be able to genuinely and openly listen. Rabbi Israel ben Eliezer, known as the *Baal Shem Tov*, said that the voice inside us never stops speaking. We need to be able to listen. In *Kabbalah* (Jewish mysticism), a person is instructed to become a vessel, a receptacle for receiving what is there. The instrument, the soul, needs to be finely tuned. One must be able to listen to the inner voice.

Many parents, consciously and unconsciously, dream many dreams about what type of children they want. Frequently, these dreams indicate that their own lives, lived vicariously through their children, were for whatever reason unable to be actualized. Sometimes the parents, who never individuated from their own parents, carry their parents' message to the third generation. What is necessary for an authentic interaction is to let go of the image of the fantasized child and to interact with the young adult that actually is. Therefore, an essential part of letting our children go is the ability to let them be. Sometimes we expect our children to make us look good to the outside world. The more they are attractive, accomplished, courteous and mentally healthy, the more it reflects upon each one of the parents and on the harmonious relationship in the home.

Erich Fromm succinctly stated that "In erotic love, two people who were separate become one. In motherly love, two people who were one become separate" (Fromm, 1958, p. 51).

D. W. Winnicott emphasizes that the mother's love and her close identification with her infant must eventually stop being all-accommodating. She must gradually be transformed into an intentionally good-enough mother to enable her children to leave in order to get some of what they need for themselves (Winnicott, 1958, pp. 223-246).

Margaret Mahler, in her seminal separation - individuating studies, found that

the emotional growth of the mother in her parenthood, her emotional willingness to let go of the toddler -- to give him, as the mother bird does, a gentle push, and encouragement toward independence is a *sine qua non* of normal (healthy) individuation. (Mahler, 1975, p. 79)

In building our own life, we emancipate ourselves from our family's myths, roles and the rigid roles of childhood. Leaving home does not become an emotional reality until we stop seeing and hearing the world through our parents' eyes.

The subjective experiences of life, our behaviors and thoughts, are governed by thousands of beliefs that comprise the map used for interpreting the events of our life. As we grow and mature, a belief that has restricted and restrained us is modified and a map of new consciousness is open to new explorations and experiments.

Defiance or compliance are not the options that define our autonomy. Autonomy is defined by the ability to actualize our free choices.

A Jewish Theory of Individuation

Is there a Jewish guideline or map towards individuation? I would like to offer a Jewish theory of individuation and of the psychological-developmental lifetime cycle based on the collective history of the Jewish people. This represents a first attempt to correlate the process of individuation with the *sequential* order of the Five Books of Moses.

Each of the Five Books of Moses is characterized by a unique theme. Genesis is known thematically as *Sefer HaYetzira*, the Book of Creation. Creation represents not only the biological creation of a new person, but the formative years of childhood and adolescence where attachment to and detachment from one's parents are already present. During this period of the first twenty years of life, some answers begin to emerge to the universal question of adolescence -- who am I? New values and commitments help us to begin to connect to our place in the wider world. The gates of Eden slowly begin to close, with feelings of nostalgia for a Golden Age that will not return. This first aspect of individuation is frequently accompanied by feelings of isolation, loneliness and confusion.

Exodus is known thematically as *Sefer HaGeulah*, the Book of Redemption.   In the process of redemption, new identifications are developed. They include attachments to one's own family and colleagues and a sense of belonging to a larger group both ethnically, culturally and professionally. New roles emerge, and abilities which were latent begin to flourish and blossom.

During this second twenty-year period, we harbor the illusion that we are really independent, only to discover our many resemblances to our parents. We discover that the angry or vindictive mother or father is really the mother or father also in ourself. Through this acknowledgment of the disquieting parental identification, we begin to liberate ourselves from some of these characteristics and develop more tolerance for some of the other characteristics.

In our marriage, parenthood and professional responsibility, we begin to grow less judgmental of the parent within us and of our real parents. This phase of our development enables us to begin to heal some of the wounds of our own childhood. Some of our childhood perceptions are recast and reframed in more reconcilable ways.   Nevertheless, the reconciliation of intergenerational family life remains imperfect and ultimately unbridgeable. Reconnected with our roots we can see ourselves; however, our relationships with our parents remain unredeemed. We become thankful for the imperfect connections and begin to focus even more on our own development as person, spouse and parent.

The third Book of the Torah, Leviticus, is known as *Sefer HaKedushah*, the Book of Holiness, the Book of Separation and the Book of Individuation. This Book of Holiness begins with "And God called" (Leviticus 1:1).   In this phase of one's life cycle, the process of individuation allows one to develop a personal relationship with God in a psychological/spiritual dimension, where God is eternally present. Carl Gustav Jung engraved on the entrance of his home, "Summoned or not, God is always present." This period's process, of being able to hear God's voice and guidance, reconnects one to the collective Divine Sinaitic Revelation on an individual basis. This period is referred to as a mid-life transition or a mid-life crisis. It is frequently ushered in by intimations of our own mortality.

Old questions assume greater significance. What is our identity? What do we want to be? Do our achievements and our goals hold value? Does our marriage make sense? Is our professional life worthwhile? What is the nature of our relationships with our family and friends? Is the God we worship a living God? Or, have we acclimated to sterile traditions and customs? Time is measured differently; we now ask how much time is left to live. Do we continue to ignore our dreams and our visions?

This process of individuation is the time of inner development. This inner development is usually marked by being less competitive and by less striving for power and external success. Turning inward may mean more focus on the home, but it primarily involves the inner development of self. We learn that we cannot necessarily change external situations, but we can reframe and change our attitudes towards those situations. This is the time that we can discuss our id, or dark side, and accept it as part of our totality. We can experience these feelings without automatically acting upon them. By tapping into our original, primitive passions at mid-life, we begin to be whole and holy. Thus, this period of God's calling and of our achieving sanctity and holiness takes place specifically when we recognize the union of opposites as part of human nature. Love and hatred, good and bad, health and illness, the angel and the devil, all become points on a continuum, rather than antitheses. We begin to integrate the feminine and masculine within ourselves. The creative and the destructive become integrated. We recognize our solitude and we crave connections. This period from 40 to 50 years of age focuses on our inner journey of becoming whole and holy.

The fourth Book of the Torah, Numbers, is known conceptually and thematically as the book of census and travels (HaPekudim). This period is concurrent with the latter phase of individuation and extends until one is approximately 70 years old. Many people pursue new projects, fulfill old dreams and enjoy more time with their families. This phase of the life cycle is frequently concerned with events not directly related to our self-interest. Can we invest ourselves in tomorrow's world? An investment in the future through leaving a legacy can enhance the quality of this period. Ego transcendence allows us to connect to the future through people and ideas. Grandparents, teachers, mentors and social reformers can leave an intellectual, spiritual and material legacy for the future.

Throughout all these travels we bring to bear the specialness which was imprinted on us in the process of individuation.

The last Book of the Torah, Deuteronomy, is known as the *Mishneh Torah* or the Book of Reminiscing. In this final period of life, we utilize our memory of our past, the feelings of the present and the anticipatory hopes for the future to take a life review of ourselves and attempt to integrate our past. We realize at this stage that we have been granted our one and only life cycle and we seek to find integrity and authenticity in the hills and valleys of our life. And even at this stage, personality changes are still possible. We can refine, revise, reframe and rearrange our tasks and our projects. This age is still part of uncharted territory, and expansion is just as possible as retraction. Our period of individuation is important in determining our capacity to change and grow in old age. Has the imminence of death become an enemy or a friend? How do we react to the ultimate separation in life as we face our own death?

Examples of Individuation

A Biblical example of the "And He called" (*VaYikra*) type of individuation is found in the First Book of Kings (19:19-21). God instructs Elijah to appoint Elisha as his prophetic successor. As Elisha is plowing, Elijah, as a messenger of God, inspires Elisha to carry his mantle.

This story illustrates how "And God called" can happen to anyone at any time, regardless of status or place. Elisha was a peasant farmer, engaged in the mundane act of plowing, when Elijah appeared to him. Rabbi Joseph B. Soloveitchik (1965) derives several lessons from this incident:

> Yet unexpectedly, the call came through to this unimaginative, self-centered farmer. Suddenly the mantle of Elijah was cast upon him. While he was engaged in the most ordinary, everyday activity, in toiling the soil, he encountered God and felt the transforming touch of God's hand. The strangest metamorphosis occurred. Within seconds, the old Elisha disappeared and a new Elisha emerged. Majestic man was replaced by covenantal man. He was initiated into a new spiritual universe in which clumsy social class distinctions had little meaning, wealth played no role, and a serene illuminated

universal "we"-consciousness supplanted the small, limited and selfish "I"-consciousness.   Old concerns changed, past commitments vanished, cherished hopes faded, and a new vision of a redemptive-covenantal reality incommensurate with the old vision of an enjoyable-majestic reality beckoned to him.   No more did the "farmer" care for the oxen, the means of making the soil yield its abundance, which were so precious to him a while ago.   No more was he concerned with anything which was so dear to him before. He slew the oxen and fed the meat to the slaves who, half-starved, toiled the soil for him and whom he, until that meeting with Elijah, had treated with contempt.   Moreover, covenantal man renounced his family relationships.   He bade farewell to father and mother and departed from their home for good.   Like his master, he became homeless.   Like his ancestor Jacob he became a "straying Aramean" who took defeat and humiliation with charity and gratitude. However, Elisha's withdrawal from majesty was not final.   He followed the dialectical course of all our prophets.   Later, when he achieved the pinnacle of faith and arrived at the outer boundaries of human commitment, he came back to society as a participant in state affairs, as an adviser of kings and a teacher of the majestic community...Elisha was indeed lonely but in his loneliness he met the Lonely One and discovered the singular covenantal confrontation of solitary man and God who abides in the recesses of transcendental solitude.   (pp. 66-67)

The process of individuation allows one to experience God during good and bad times.   An example of individuation under duress is found in the writings of Etty Hillesum (1986).   Born in 1914, Etty Hillesum was a Dutch Jew who spent the last months of her life in Westerbork, a transit camp in the Netherlands for those being transported to Auschwitz.   There she kept a diary and nursed the sick in the hospital barracks.   As she was being deported to Auschwitz in 1943, she wrote a note on a scrap of paper expressing the feeling that although she knew what would befall her and her people, she was able to sing.   Her soul was able to expand and say to God that she was grateful for her life; and when some of her relatives and friends died or were murdered, she was able to not only mourn the loss, but also to relish and cherish the time they were able to be together.   Etty Hillesum had individuated and she was able to sing.   Etty Hillesum endured tremendous suffering, but she was able to transform the pain and suffering and created an even closer relationship with God.

On August 18, 1943, in Westerbork she wrote:

> You have made me so rich, oh God, please let me share out Your beauty with open hands. My life has become an uninterrupted dialogue with You, oh God, one great dialogue. Sometimes when I stand in some corner of the camp, my feet planted on Your earth, my eyes raised toward Your heaven, tears sometimes run down my face, tears of deep emotion and gratitude. At night, too, when I lie in my bed and rest in You, oh God, tears of gratitude run down my face, and that is my prayer. I have been terribly tired for several days, but that too will pass. Things come and go in a deeper rhythm, and people must be taught to *listen*; it is the most important thing we have to learn in this life. I am not challenging You, oh God, my life is one great dialogue with You. I may never become the great artist I would really like to be, but I am already secure in You, God. Sometimes I try my hand at turning out small profundities and uncertain short stories, but I always end up with just one single word: God. And that says everything and there is no need for anything more. And all my creative powers are translated into inner dialogues with You. The beat of my heart has grown deeper, more active, and yet more peaceful, and it is as if I were all the time storing up inner riches. (Hillesum, 1986, p. 116)

Sometimes, this awakening through individuation comes after a tremendous shock in a person's life. I recently visited a 65-year-old comatose female who fell into an irreversible coma when an unanticipated post-operative complication took place after a fairly routine surgery. The husband was sitting next to his wife in an intensive care unit, holding her hand with love, compassion and tears. On subsequent visits, the identical situation presented itself. On one occasion, the husband turned to me and said the following, more or less, with tear-filled eyes:

> You know, Rabbi Meier, I really was not existing until my wife fell into a coma. I always loved my wife and children and we had a nice life, perhaps something like the average American Jewish family. But now, I have held her hand with more intensity than ever before.

I have spent more quality time without distractions and interruptions than in the past thirty years. The intensity and the realization of my individual existence and my love for my wife have never been as great as they are now, when it is too late. Why did I individuate so late in life and after this tragedy? Why did I not realize what my life was and what my life is?

Sometimes, acts of individuation can be sparked by quiet meditation. A story is told about a certain mountaineer who stayed on top of a mountain for a week at a time in quiet contemplation and complete relaxation. Each week, he would descend from the mountain to purchase the next week's supplies with the limited money he had. One day, as he was leaving the store, he noticed an eagle in a cage. He asked the owner of the store the price of the eagle and, realizing that he did not have enough money, returned all the supplies to the owner and purchased the eagle. He left the store, opened the cage and let the eagle fly, saying that eagles are meant to fly. He echoed the thoughts of William Blake that "No bird soars too high, if he soars with his own wings" (Blake, 1966). Liberating the eagle demonstrated the mountaineer's sensitivity to his surroundings and his ability to sacrifice finances and even basic necessities to implement his lofty goal and objective. When the eagle was liberated, the mountaineer's soul was climbing the ladder of ascension to be united with God.

Individuation and *Shema Yisroel*

One of the first prayers a child is taught is the *Shema Yisroel* ("Hear, O Israel;" Deuteronomy 6:4), the Jewish declaration of faith. The last prayer which a Jew recites before death is the *Shema Yisroel*. Is there a special meaning to this prayer that relates to the process of individuation, whereby every Jew can develop so that "And He called" (Leviticus 1:1) can apply to everyone?

Rabbi Adolf (Avraham) Altmann, the former Chief Rabbi of Trier, Germany, derived a number of special meanings from the *Shema* (Altmann, 1928). (For a brief biography of Rabbi Altmann and the complete text of his article on the *Shema*, see the following chapter.) Rabbi Altmann learned numerous lessons from the phraseology of the *Shema*. He highlighted the significance of the first word of this prayer, asking why the sense of *hearing* was selected to declare our faith, and he shows how it addresses itself continuously to individuals and to the Jewish people.

Rabbi Altmann states:

> According to the Bible, at Sinai, God revealed Himself to the Israelites directly, through the voice which they heard. Consequently, through the sense of hearing they became convinced of God's existence in a direct, concrete way. The Jewish declaration of faith ties in with this, as if to say: "Israel, you who once heard with your own ears the voice of God from Horeb, hear that same supernatural sound reverberate within you, hear eternally the Eternal, your God, speak to you." And so it is that the summons, taken up from the unique context of Moses' farewell speech, grows into something that transcends the senses of the generation of that time and speaks to Jewish generations down the millennia with the force of an unquenchable fire: "Hear, O Israel! Hear evermore the voice of God that once resounded and since then is reproduced, eternally new, creatively within! Experience God ever again concretely through the inner ear, as if you were perpetually listening to the original sound."

As a result of this new interpretation, the *Shema* can now be translated in an alternative manner:

> "Hear, O Israel, the Eternal, our God: The Eternal is the Unique One." (Altmann, 1928)

This ability to listen and to hear allows the voice of God to be heard continually on a daily basis. This is a central aspect of individuation.

> In the declaration of faith of the uninterrupted hearing of God, one finds not only the point of origin of Jewish faith, but also a source of strength in regard to practical ethics. Hearing God, this act which renders the religious attitude eternally new, lends the commandments of the Torah an incomparable vitality and freshness. If Israel can hear their God speak to them daily through the words of the *Shema*, they also will hear, every day, what it is that God has to say to them. Each commandment is a living transference of the voice of God that Israel once heard loud and clear. That is what Moses meant when,

as an introduction to his report of the act of revelation on Sinai, he summoned all of Israel and said: "*Hear, O Israel*, the statutes and judgments which I speak in your ears this day" (Deuteronomy 5:1), and it was on this that he based his further assertion, "not only with our ancestors has God made this covenant, but also with us, we who are all of us alive this day" (Deuteronomy 5:3). (Altmann, 1928)

This hearing also has an ethical dimension.

If no one else hears the silent cry of the humiliated, the powerless hidden victims, the Jew must hear it; that is the noblest ethical significance of the "Hear, O Israel." Through the silent walls of hard prison cells hear the sighs, Israel; out of the lonely huts of deserted widows and orphans, from the bed of pain of the sick and suffering, from the silently borne anguish of those rejected or denied justice; from the mute looks of the timid and sorrow-laden, from the pale lips of the starving and needy, you as a Jew must hear the cries of pain, without their having to be emitted. The cry of suffering is the cry of God, calling out from its victims to you. As the Psalmist lets God speak: "With the oppressed, I am one in suffering" (Psalms 91:15). (Altmann, 1928)

Even beyond the ethical domain, the ultimate meaning of the *Shema* is that true listening and hearing should be done with one's heart, as one re-experiences Revelation.

To read the *Shema* properly -- the Sages tell us -- means to direct the *Kavvanah* (intention) of the heart toward it. This duty applies in particular to the first sentence of the declaration of faith. The ear must hear the language of the lips when the *Shema* is read, but the heart must be the real ear. To be truly filled with the spiritual insight and ethical contents of the *Shema Yisroel* bids one, however, to experience in oneself the wellspring of this belief and this ethic, to consider oneself ever again before Sinai and hearing God's voice speak. The *Shema* is thus the most profound Jewish fundamental truth, in the sense that the greatest concepts of Judaism are expressed within it. Revelation, awareness of God and ethics constitute the meaning and soul of the "Hear, O Israel." (Altmann, 1928)

Individuation and Death

Death is not only the final moment in life, but is also the last stage of growth and development. The final prayer that is recited before death is the *Shema Yisroel*. Even in the moment of death, we are called upon to hear God's revelation.

Shema - throughout life and even at this moment of death, we hear the voice of God. We reminisce about our past and anticipate an unknown but very real spiritual future life. We are cognizant that this very moment is a moment of ultimate preparation. The way we approach death may indeed have an impact on the type of spiritual life that awaits us. And we end with *Ehad* (Oneness and Unity). All the mysteries and challenges of life, all our experiences, visions, fantasies and dreams, all the art, music, and poetry, all of our ancestors and our family that remains become a unified whole and one. Through this lifelong process of becoming and individuating, we become one with ourselves and one with God.

References

Altmann, Adolf (Avraham). (1928). Sinn und Seele des "Höre Israel." ("The Meaning and Soul of 'Hear, O Israel'"). Berlin: *Jeschurun* (ed. by Joseph Wohlgemuth), *11/12*. Translated from the German by Barbara R. Algin (1991), published in English in this volume.

Blake, W. (1966). *The complete writings of William Blake*, edited by Geoffrey Keynes. Oxford: Oxford University Press.

Fromm, E. (1950). *Psychoanalysis and religion.* New Haven: Yale University Press.

Fromm, E. (1956). *The art of loving.* New York: Harper & Brothers.

Guntrip, H. (1969). *Schizoid phenomenon, objects relations, and the self.* New York: International Universities Press.

Hillesum, E. (1985). *An interrupted life: The diaries of Etty Hillesum, 1941-43.* New York: Pocket Books.

Hillesum, E. (1986). *Letters from Westerbork.* New York: Pantheon Books.

The Holy Scriptures. (2 vols.) (1917). Philadelphia: Jewish Publication Society.

Jung, C.G. (1970). *Collected works.* Princeton: Princeton University Press.

Kuhn, T. (1970). 2nd ed. *The structure of scientific revolutions.* Chicago: University of Chicago Press.

Mahler, M., Pine, F., and Bergman, A. (1975). *The psychological birth of the human infant.* New York: Basic Books.

Meany, J. (1988). Jungian psychology and the Jesus prayer. In J.M. Spiegelman. (Ed.) *Catholicism and Jungian psychology.* Phoenix: Falcon Press.

Meier, L. (1988). The loneliness-togetherness dialectic: A psycho-Judaic perspective. In L. Meier. *Jewish values in psychotherapy: Essays on vital issues on the search for meaning.* Lanham, Md.: University Press of America.

Midrash (10 vols.). (1961). H. Freedman and M. Simons (Eds.). London: Soncino Press.

Soloveitchik, J.B. (1965). The lonely man of faith. *Tradition, 7(2),* 5-67.

Spero, M.H. (1985). *Psychotherapy of the religious patient.* Springfield, Ill.: Charles C. Thomas.

The Talmud. (18 vols.). (1961). I. Epstein (Ed.). London: Soncino Press.

Talmud (Jerusalem). (5 vols.). (1960). New York: Otzar Hasefarim.

Winnicott, D.W. (1958). *Collected papers.* New York: Basic Books.

Introductory Note to Chapter III

Rabbi Altmann's article on "Hear, O Israel" originally appeared in German as "Sinn und Seele des 'Höre Israel'" ("The Meaning and Soul of 'Hear, O Israel'"). The German article was published in Berlin in *Jeschurun*, number 11/12 (1928), edited by Joseph Wohlgemuth. I am indebted to Dr. Manfred Altman of London for his encouragement and guidance in producing an English translation of this seminal article.

Rabbi Altmann's article follows the chapter on "Individuation and *Shema Yisroel* (Hear, O Israel)." His article serves as a further exposition of this concept, clarifying how individuals, as they go through life, continue to hear different aspects of divine revelation, which is eternal. Rabbi Altmann's article, with its novel interpretation, is one of the best explanations of the basis of faith, as expressed in the *Shema*. It is an honor and privilege to present his article in English for the first time, so that it can reach the wide audience it deserves.

Rabbi Dr. Adolf (Avraham) Altmann, the former Chief Rabbi of Trier, Germany, was also an eminent historian, philosopher and theologian. He was a prolific author and orator who participated widely in Jewish cultural life in Austria and Germany. An early follower of Herzl, he was a delegate to the First Mizrahi Congress in Pressburg. In World War I, Rabbi Altmann served as senior chaplain in the Austro-Hungarian Army, receiving the Golden Cross of Merit. In 1956, a street was named after him in Trier, and in 1979, in commemoration of the centenary of his birth, a special ceremony was held in that city's Town Hall and a brochure on this event was published by the City of Trier.

In 1989, a street was named after him in Salzburg, Austria. His still authoritative work, "History of the Jews in City and Country of Salzburg," has been officially republished with the inclusion of a biographical survey on his life and work by his son Dr. Manfred Altman (Otto Muller Verlag, Salzburg, 1990; in German, with bibliography of Rabbi Altmann's works and of literature on him). An official ceremony was held in Salzburg to mark these events.

An article in the *Encyclopaedia Judaica Year Book* (Jerusalem, 1983-5) gives information on the life of this illustrious communal leader. For more information about Rabbi Altmann, refer to Alexander Altmann's "Adolf Altmann: A Filial Memoir," Leo Baeck Yearbook XXVI, 1981, Leo Baeck Institute, London.

Rabbi Altmann and his wife, along with many members of their family, were saintly martyrs of the Holocaust during World War II. Their youngest son, Wilhelm, after graduating with honors as a chemical engineer at Delft University, Holland, endeavored to join the French Resistance, was caught, taken to Drancy Concentration Camp early in July, 1942, and was deported to Auschwitz, where he was killed on July 30, 1942. Their daughter, Hilda, and her family were deported from Westerbork to Auschwitz on September 7, 1943, on the same transport train as Etty Hillesum, whose writings are quoted in the preceding chapter. Rabbi Avraham Altmann and his wife, Malvine, née Weisz, were deported from Westerbork to Theresienstadt in February, 1944, and in May, 1944, to Auschwitz, where they perished. A fellow inmate there, Rabbi Dr. B. Gottschall, survived and reported how in the midst of Rabbi Altmann's illness, hunger and humiliation, his faith and spiritual uplift never left him. His wife shared in this heroic stance (see pages 166-7 of Alexander Altmann's "Filial Memoir"). Their sons Alexander and Manfred survived, as they were in England, and their son Erwin survived, as he was in the United States when Holland was invaded. All rescue efforts were in vain.

In Etty Hillesum's book, *Letters from Westerbork* (1986), she wrote (p. 132): "I see a dying man being carried away reciting the Sh'ma to himself." Her observation illustrates the centrality and the significance of the *Shema* in all times and in all situations.

Chief Rabbi Dr. Adolf (Avraham) Altmann
Photo by courtesy of
Manfred Altman, London

THE MEANING AND SOUL OF "HEAR, O ISRAEL"

by the late Dr. Adolf (Avraham) Altmann
Chief Rabbi, Trier (Germany)

Translation from German by Dr. Barbara R. Algin
Edited by Rabbi Levi Meier, Ph.D.

CHAPTER III

THE MEANING AND SOUL OF "HEAR, O ISRAEL"

Our Jewish declaration of faith, "Hear, O Israel, the Eternal is our God, the Eternal is the Unique One" (Deuteronomy 6:4), is like other declarations of faith, the formal expression of an insight and the formula for expressing awareness of its basis. We discern and know that the Eternal is our God, and we share this awareness with one another by proclaiming "Hear, O Israel." But what is the essence of this insight, its soul? How is it gained and what is its essential core? This is apparently not communicated. Only one facet, insight, is communicated; but there is nothing to tell us how it came about. Are we perhaps dealing with nothing more than an axiomatic metaphysical statement? Were that the case, it would not be an insight that could justify its final definitive formulation and the conviction it expresses of its validity. If its source is to be found in a philosophical-logical inference, what would this be? Or is the insight, the awareness, perhaps founded on an experience, on a sensory perception? With this latter assumption, we probably come nearest to understanding the meaning and power of conviction of our declaration of faith[1]. It will be shown that the formulation of the declaration does not only communicate the insight itself, but also communicates its source, so that we have the meaning and soul of the declaration at the same time.

The formula of the declaration introduces its basic content of faith with an imperative, with the entreaty "Hear!" What is the point of this demand, what purpose has this imperative "Hear!"? The commentaries are silent about this word. Only Rabbi Obadiah ben Jacob Sforno in his Torah commentary takes notice of it. He understands the meaning of the word simply as a call to pay attention to the impending message -- "take notice and comprehend this: the Eternal is our God, the Eternal is the One!" However, this explanation can hardly exhaust the meaning of the word in this context. When we refer to something concrete or factually present, a requirement to pay particular attention to what is under discussion is warranted, in order to gain insights through accurate perception (e.g.

Deuteronomy 9:1; 20:3)[2]. However, where it concerns, as in our situation, the imparting of a metaphysical concept, an introductory appeal to be attentive is not understandable; it has no meaning, because however intensive the attention may be, it does not add anything new to the sources of the insight, which are supposed to nurture the conviction. In such a case, the reminder to be attentive would have to be described as an irrelevant introduction. This appeal does not contribute to a strengthening and enhancement of the insight, voiced in the declaration of faith[3]. Therefore, it would have been sufficient to give only the pure message: the Eternal is our God, the Eternal is the Unique One.

Evidently, then, "Hear, O Israel" is more than a mere call to attention. This imperative must, perhaps, in itself indicate the source of comprehension of the contents of the teachings that it introduces. In fact, it is an appeal directed to one of the senses -- a source of awareness, not of a conceptual kind, but rather one that is sense-communicated, almost concrete. Apparently, the awareness that the Torah propounds is an awareness based upon experience: the Jewish potential for spiritual awareness is called upon to experience in life the fact that the Eternal is our God and One; and that awareness is particularly linked to the capacity of one of the senses to convey to the Jew the awareness of God. How this is meant to operate and what Israel is supposed to hear in order to give form to their awareness of God will be shown. It will emerge from the answer to a question that is still open -- why is it that the sense of hearing is selected to express the call? If the sensory perception is supposed to be a source for awareness of God, why should it be limited to the sense of hearing? Equally, could not and should not every tree and every shrub that comes into our field of vision, every flower and every blossom giving us fragrance, everything that we eat, perceived by our taste, everything tangible making itself known to our sense of touch, give us evidence of God's, the Creator's existence? Every look upward toward the blue sky, toward the radiant sun, toward the gleaming stars; every look downward, toward the fertile earth, toward the beauty of nature, toward life at its most triumphant -- if experience is meant to contribute to the awareness of God -- should be potentially no less effective, no less clear an intimation of God than sound, the music of nature, conveyed to the ear.

The question is even more justifiable since, after all, the Bible itself appeals to the evidence of other senses to perceive God's existence (e.g.,

Psalms 34:9). The Bible is especially rich in narrative and other passages which refer to seeing as the source of the conviction of God's existence and His omnipotence. From this enormous wealth of texts[4], the following may be cited: "For you it has been shown that you might know that the Eternal is God, there is no one except Him" (Deuteronomy 4:35); "See now that I, even I, am He, and there is no god with Me" (Deuteronomy 32:39)[5]. Do these quotes not also authenticate vision, alongside hearing, as a source of awareness of God? Indeed, these passages might just as well have become Israel's declaration of faith, since they contain essentially the same assertion, of God's existence and uniqueness. And yet it was the sentence, "Hear, O Israel, the Eternal is our God, the Eternal is One," that alone has become Israel's declaration of faith, and only hearing is expressed as the source of sensory perception through which awareness of God is attained. Why is this so? Could the text not just as well have said accurately "See, Israel" instead of "Hear," or as occurs once in Ezekiel (44:5), both "see" and "hear" together? Clearly, hearing has been quite deliberately chosen as the only appropriate sensory analogy and the essence of the Jewish awareness of God is integrally bound up with the faculty of hearing. In a certain sense the imperative "Hear" proves, as it were, the truth of the metaphysical statement about God.

This is the reason why only this sentence, and no other, has been chosen to be the sentence of the declaration of faith. And which hearing is meant here should not be subject to doubt. In the central position that the fact of divine revelation assumes in Judaism, the cardinal sentence of the Jewish religion -- the fundamental statement of belief concerning the essence of God -- points to the act of revelation as the channel through which awareness of God's existence is imparted and assured with convincing force. According to the Bible, at Sinai, God revealed Himself to the Israelites directly, through the voice which they heard. Consequently, through the sense of hearing they became convinced of God's existence in a direct, concrete way. The Jewish declaration of faith ties in with this, as if to say: "Israel, you who once heard with your own ears the voice of God from Horeb, hear that same supernatural sound reverberate within you, hear eternally the Eternal, your God, speak to you." And so it is that the summons, taken up from the unique context of Moses' farewell speech, grows into something that transcends the senses of the generation of that time and speaks to Jewish generations down the millennia with the force of an unquenchable fire: "Hear, O Israel! Hear evermore the voice of God that once resounded and since then is reproduced, eternally new, creatively within! Experience God ever again concretely through the inner ear, as if you were perpetually listening to the original sound."

Israel could, to be sure, infer the existence of God, their God, from experiences communicated by the other senses as well. From the miracles which they could see, to the manna which they were allowed to savor, everything pointed to the existence of a caring, great and mighty God, who dwelled among them and hovered above them. But all that, however, meant only a discovery of God through inferences and deductions, not much different from purely logical speculation, in the course of which refutation and conceptual variation can be expected. What Israel saw with their own eyes gave them proof of God's existence; what they *heard* at Mount Sinai emanated directly from God. That is, as Judah Halevi put it in his *Kuzari*, in order to prevent anthropomorphic interpretation, God brought about the physiological impression of a voice (Deuteronomy 4:12, 15), but only of a voice. As Moses later reminded them: "The sound of the words you heard, only sounds, but you saw no picture" (*Kuzari* I:89, English translation, H. Hirschfeld, 2nd ed., 1931, p. 55); "you saw no picture at all, when the Lord spoke to you on Horeb from the middle of the fire." All the passages from the Torah which use the imperative for the sense of vision or other senses to recognize God could therefore not become the sentence of the declaration of faith -- however much they expressed the same content as our sentence under discussion. And that text again could select no other appeal to the senses than the imperative "Hear!," since the declaration of faith links up with the immediate awareness of God attained by Israel in the most concrete manner feasible, through listening[6]. The Jew is to *hear* the Eternal, his God, and recognize while hearing that He exists, and exists as uniquely the ONE[7].

Each morning, when the Jew receives his soul anew, each evening, when he entrusts it into God's hand, when his heart is bursting with joy or contracting in grief; as a child, when his father teaches it to him as the first sounds that he learns, and as an old man for whom funeral candles seem ready to be lit; on an ordinary work day, or on Yom Kippur in the deepest devotion of the Day of Atonement -- on all these occasions, the declaration of faith must, for a Jew, mean the experience of feeling himself in spirit standing at Sinai and, as it were, allowing God to speak directly to him, as Isaiah puts it: "He wakes morning by morning, he wakes my ear to hear, like they who are taught" (Isaiah 50:4). The *Midrash Rabbah* to

Deuteronomy seems to hint at the same idea: "From where does Israel have the privilege to recite the *Shema*? Rabbi Pinhas bar Hama said, from the act of revelation at Sinai, where God Himself uttered the *Shema*. Before beginning 'I am the Eternal, your God,' He called: 'Hear, O Israel,' and all affirmed: 'The Eternal is our God, the Eternal is One[8].'"

We must, then, translate our declaration of faith differently from what has until now been its conventional reading. Not "Hear, O Israel; the Eternal is our God, the Eternal is One," that is, divided into two parts, one introductory ("Hear, O Israel") and the second part containing two separate statements ("the Eternal is our God; the Eternal is One"). Nor again by a facile simplification of the second part that would construe *Elohenu*, our God, as being in apposition to the Eternal, as appears in various German (Zunz, Philippson, Hirsch and Bernfeld) and other translations. Either everything that follows "*Shema Yisroel*" has to be treated as the object of the verb, "*shema*," yielding "Hear, O Israel, the Eternal, our God, the Eternal, the Unique One," or the first clause only of the second part is to be considered the object of the verb, its second clause being a separate statement. Thus, "Hear, O Israel, the Eternal, our God: The Eternal is the Unique One[9]."

This, so to speak, uninterrupted hearing of God is often found wonderfully allegorized in the phraseology of our tradition. Thus, Rabbi Joshua ben Levi speaks in the *Ethics of the Fathers* of the divine echo (*bat kol*) that reverberates daily from Horeb[10]. God's Sinai voice has never turned silent for us[11]; its echo continues throughout time. Only through this continued, inner, intuitive receptivity to that divine voice has Israel's belief in God remained free of any dilution by visual representation. For this reason, Moses warned his people with reference to God's voice, heard by Israel: "Only be very much on your guard, that you do not make yourself a picture of God, because you have seen no picture and no form, only heard a voice when the Lord spoke to you" (see Deuteronomy 4:12-19).

Sound stands nearest to the purely spiritual among the phenomena of the world of the senses. Therefore, God has chosen it to be the medium of sensory revelation. Since what is heard is the least dimensional, it is easier to imagine it as something unlimited, and extendable into infinity, than what is visible or tactile. Sense and spirit mutually interact in hearing. Through Israel's capacity to listen, God's self-revelation was concretized, and its spirit remained protected from crudely superficial representation. In this, not only God's existence is expressed, but also His Oneness. Idols can be seen, touched and perceived in other ways as well, even though as both Moses and David mockingly observed, they can do none of these things themselves. One can perceive them, but one cannot hear an idol speak. Through hearing God, Israel became convinced not only of His existence but of His uniqueness. As Moses emphasized, "did ever a people hear the voice of God as you have heard it and live?" (Deuteronomy 4:33, 5:23)

In the declaration of faith of the uninterrupted hearing of God, one finds not only the point of origin of Jewish faith, but also a source of strength in regard to practical ethics. Hearing God, this act which renders the religious attitude eternally new, lends the commandments of the Torah an incomparable vitality and freshness. If Israel can hear their God speak to them daily through the words of the *Shema*, they also will hear, every day, what it is that God has to say to them. Each commandment is a living transference of the voice of God that Israel once heard loud and clear. That is what Moses meant when, as an introduction to his report of the act of revelation on Sinai, he summoned all of Israel and said: "*Hear, O Israel*, the statutes and judgments which I speak in your ears this day" (Deuteronomy 5:1), and it was on this that he based his further assertion, "not only with our ancestors has God made this covenant, but also with us, we who are all of us alive this day" (Deuteronomy 5:3). If the voice from Sinai ever ceases for us, so will the life-pervading content of its message, and our ethical being will fade away. Only because the *Shema* is an invitation to experience anew, to listen to the voice that we once experienced at Sinai, can the most difficult religious moral demand -- to love God with our whole heart, our whole soul and all possessions -- follow immediately as self-evident.

Only the non-rational recreation and deepest reexperiencing of the most powerful religious primal experience offers basis and assurance for realizing this ethical task. "Hear, O Israel" is therefore simultaneously both God-awareness and ethic. *Na'aseh ve-Nishmah*[12], the deed of obedience resulting from hearing God, is not only obedience to God, but also the human listening response. Out of the call of another human being, God's voice can also speak to us. As the Sages teach, God's voice itself spoke to the people in the words and directives of Moses, just as God had assured him immediately when He commissioned him for his task: "I will be with your mouth and will teach you what you shall say" (Exodus 4:12)[13]. While calling Moses out of the burning bush, God's voice disguised itself as that of Moses' father, Amram, in order to speak even more intimately to Moses' soul. The *Shema* reminds us, according to the moralizing version of the Midrash (Genesis *Rabbah* 2:3), to be prepared to recognize God's voice sounding through the voices of those who speak to us for God and in His name. The daily recitation of the *Shema* by Israel, the descendants of Jacob, also ties in with the affirmation of it by his own sons, addressed to him when he gathered them around prior to his death and challenged them with the ultimate question -- whether or not their hearts were, and would remain, undividedly loyal to God, the Uniquely-One. In reply, they exclaimed: "Hear, O Israel, our father: just as in your heart there is room only for the Uniquely-One, so it is in ours, too." Reassured, the patriarch departed this life, with the praise of God on his lips, and our daily *Shema* calls out to him, saying: "Hear, Israel, you who are at rest in the cave of Machpelah, the heritage to which your call to remember obligated us then is still alive in us; the Eternal, our God, is for us the Uniquely-One." Even though, cognitively, "Hear, O Israel" focuses on the direct hearing of the voice of God from Sinai, it also includes in ethical-practical terms, this indirect listening to God; it wants to educate man to become an ethically attentive human being.

There are voices and calls which sound out loud, yet one fails to hear them, and there are others that make no sound at all, yet they are heard. The human without ethics passes by what cries out most in life without hearing, whereas one of high moral character hears even the most subdued call and traces its source. He knows that what is most quiet sometimes speaks loudest. Often something cries out powerfully toward heaven, just because it makes less noise, as did the voice of Abel's silent blood, shed by his brother (Genesis 4:10). If no one else hears the silent cry of the humiliated, the powerless hidden victims, the Jew must hear it; that is the noblest ethical significance of the "Hear, O Israel." Through the silent walls of hard prison cells hear the sighs, Israel; out of the lonely huts of deserted widows and orphans, from the bed of pain of the sick and suffering, from the silently borne anguish of those rejected or denied justice; from the mute looks of the timid and sorrow-laden, from the pale lips of the starving and needy, you as a Jew must hear the cries of pain, without their having to be emitted. The cry of suffering is the cry of God, calling out from its victims to you. As the Psalmist lets God speak: "With the oppressed, I am one in suffering" (Psalms 91:15).

A poet should be required to try to describe that quiet but primal cry which, unheard by those of coarse sensitivity, constantly penetrates through God's nature admonishingly from heaven to earth and speaks in silence, the strongest language. A painter dips his brush in the strongest colors and produces something that depicts the thousand nuances of the dumb shriek of blood and misery, an appeal whose silent eeriness reaches from earth to heaven. The sculptor, on the other hand, can use his chisel to fashion a human figure which, reaching up to heaven while also being directed intimately toward earth, expresses symbolically the connection between what is above and what is below, a figure that embodies the triumph over the silent cry attained by simply responding to it.

But even without artistry, every Jew may gain an ethical triumph in the here and now and have it imprinted on his soul -- through his *Shema Yisroel.* Art is only suggestion; experience, however, is fulfillment, and "Hear, O Israel" is experience.

The universe is filled with voices, but only those attuned will hear them. "The heavens declare the glory of God," the Psalmist sings, "and the firmament announces the work of His hand. Day to day utters speech, and night to night expresses knowledge. There is no speech nor are there words; their voice is not heard" (Psalms 19:2-4).

What does man, whose awareness is subject to the restraint of the world of senses, know of things that hover between heaven and earth, regarding which his book learning cannot even teach him to dream?

Radio has been discovered in our time. Voices float through space on waves that pass through the ether. They flow mute and silent in their course; no one hears them, but they are there. If one employs the proper apparatus for attracting and amplifying them, we can detect them, and they become audible. Engineers from the famous Marconi company -- as I read some time ago -- have discovered through experiment the astonishing fact that their apparatus makes it possible to receive broadcast music even after it has been carried on waves three times the distance of the earth's circumference. This discovery has raised the question, in the world of science, as to whether sound waves can ever be lost. According to the law of conservation of energy, it should theoretically be possible -- so the argument runs -- to devise instruments of such highly refined sensitivity as to render audible waves carrying sound that was heard loud many years ago and which are still moving through space, so that -- in theory -- voices from remote antiquity could be conjured up out of the ether.

God's voice of revelation cannot have become audible only once for all time. It is not lost, just as the cry of every creature in the universe is there, even though it appears to be silent. But one has no need of artificial, external aids to perceive it. If the Jew applies his heart to things that concern faith and that concern life, if he inclines his inner ear with its specific sensitivity, he will hear the voices. That is the meaning of a Talmudic saying in relation to the Scriptural verse: "And He said: 'When you will listen to the voice of the Eternal, of your God'..." (Exodus 15:26; *Berakhot* 40a; *Sukkah* 46b). "When you will hear" is, as often in the Torah, also expressed here with the double words *Shamoa Tishma*, which mean: If you, with finely tuned hearing of the heart, turn to listen to that ancient voice, you will hear it ever again renewed, but if you turn your heart from it, then you will not hear it anymore.

Several of the major interpreters of Jewish tradition observe that the recitation of the *Shema* is a kind of daily attestation by the Jew to the significance of God and Israel, and at the same time a daily renewal of God's witnessing for Israel. For this reason, the *Ayin* and *Dalet* at the end of the words *Shema* and *Ehad* are written in capital letters in the Torah. Together, these letters make the word *Ed*, "witness"[14]. One who utters the *Shema* is simultaneously acknowledging: "I hear, I am witness;" and saying "You be witness too and hear."

But to be witness in hearing one must really hear, otherwise one is a false witness. How can one direct the inner ear above all foreign outside noise toward the ancient voice calling from Sinai? The answer is, with the heart.

To read the *Shema* properly -- the Sages tell us -- means to direct the *Kavvanah* (intention) of the heart toward it. This duty applies in particular to the first sentence of the declaration of faith[15]. The ear must hear the language of the lips when the *Shema* is read[16], but the heart must be the real ear. To be truly filled with the spiritual insight and ethical contents of the *Shema Yisroel* bids one, however, to experience in oneself the wellspring of this belief and this ethic, to consider oneself ever again before Sinai and hearing God's voice speak. The *Shema* is thus the most profound Jewish fundamental truth, in the sense that the greatest concepts of Judaism are expressed within it. Revelation, awareness of God and ethics constitute the meaning and soul of the "Hear, O Israel."

Notes

*The word "Eternal" has been used instead of the word "Lord," in accordance with the correct translation of the German, *der Ewige*.

[1]cf. Babylonian Talmud, *Pesahim* 56a (English translation, The Soncino Talmud, ed. I. Epstein) (Rashi and *Tosafot*). The first verse of the *Shema* is to be understood neither as a command nor as a prayer to God, but as a spontaneous acknowledgement, and it is as such that it is to be recited.

[2]In such cases the imperative *shema, hear*, frequently occurs.

[3]At *Deuteronomy* 4:1 and 5:1, the imperative *shema* is used to express both obedience and internalization: "now, therefore, hear, O Israel, the statutes...". It should be noted that laws are factual items, to some extent corresponding to actuality, and that appeal to take note of them does not presuppose any purely insight-oriented approach. At *Deuteronomy* 27:9 *shema* is supplemented (and thus semantically affected) by *hasket* so as to mean *attend*, in order to impress the actuality of a specific event upon Israel's awareness the more forcibly. Where appeal is made, as in the passage under discussion, for acknowledgement, "hear" is dispensed with, and the imperative of the verb *yada*, "know, be apprised of," is used: *Psalms* 46:11, "know that I am God;" *1 Chronicles* 28:9, "know thou the God of thy father." The verb to *see*, in place of to *hear*, is also frequently used when the appeal is directed to the recognition of God. See further below in the text.

[4]e.g., *Genesis* 18,1; 32:31; *Exodus* 16:7; 20:22; 24:10; 34:10; *Leviticus* 9:4; *Numbers* 14:14, 22; *Deuteronomy* 4:9, 35; 5:21; 32:39; *1 Kings* 22:19; *Isaiah* 6:1; 35:2; 40:26; *Jeremiah* 31:3; *Ezekiel* 1:1; *Zechariah* 9:14; *Psalms* 97:6; *Job* 42:5; *2 Chronicles* 18:18; 26:5.

[5]Here the imperative is used, as in the case of *shema, hear*.

[6]Despite the fact that this notion, as the quintessence of the *Shema*, grows out of the spirit of basic Jewish teaching, surprisingly it is not mentioned even *en passant* by any of the commentators on *Deuteronomy* 6:4. It is only S.R. Hirsch who glances at it in his commentary to the

Pentateuch, without however either drawing the full conclusions or anchoring it in his translation of the text. He merely remarks that prior to the giving of the Torah at Sinai, only the idiom of vision was used to describe the source of Israel's awareness of God, and only subsequently thereto the idiom of hearing.

[7]This gives a deeper meaning to the view of Judah the Prince, R. Yose, and R. Judah bar Ilai in the Babylonian Talmud, *Berakhot* 13a and 15a-b, according to whom when reading the *Shema* it is obligatory to articulate it in sound that the ear can sense, although in the case of other precepts this is unnecessary. Although the canonical ruling (*halakhah*) is not absolutely firm behind this opinion, it does hold that in principle the *Shema* is to be recited aloud. In particular the cantor or other prayer-leader must read it aloud for the congregation, so that the meaning of the word *Shema* (*hear*) may be reflected in practice when the commandment to recite it is fulfilled. See Maimonides, *Hilkhot Keriyat Shema*, 2:8; *Shulhan Arukh, Orah Hayyim* 61:4, 26; 62:3, 5.

[8]*Midrash Rabbah*, (English translation, The Soncino Midrash, ed. H. Freedman and M. Simon), *Deuteronomy* 2:31 (on 6:4). *Ibid.*, 35 another reason is cited for Israel being privileged to read the *Shema*. Before his death, the patriarch Jacob gathered his sons around him and gave vent to misgivings lest they might turn to other gods after he was dead. At which they unanimously exclaimed "Hear, O Israel (our father), the Eternal is our God, the Eternal is for us the only God," and Jacob added, in an undertone, "Blessed be the Name of His glorious kingdom for ever and ever." On this Rabbi Levi remarked that ever since, when reciting the *Shema*, Jews have associated with it the sense "Hear, Israel, our ancestor: that same heritage regarding which You did enjoin us we still preserve today; the Eternal is our God, the Eternal is One." Somewhat differently, but on similar lines, *Midrash Rabbah, Genesis* 98:3; cf. also *Sifre, Deuteronomy* on 6:4; and the Babylonian Talmud, *Pesahim* 56a. The latter source does not link the institution of the reciting of the *Shema* itself with the Jacob episode, but only the insertion, after the introductory verse, of the words "Blessed be the Name of His glorious kingdom for ever and ever;" and it is significant that Maimonides (*Hilkhot Keriyat Shema* 1:4) mentions this in his code merely as the reason that gives authority for saying these words silently, after the introductory sentence of the *Shema*. cf. *Kesef Mishneh*, ad loc. It is also noteworthy that the talmudic passage, taken up by Maimonides (*Pesahim*

56a) explains that the first sentence, *Shema* ("hear," etc.), which emanates from Moses and is written in the Torah must, as such, be spoken aloud, but that the utterance merely traditionally ascribed to Jacob is not. This is proof that *Deuteronomy* 6:4 itself, with all that is implicit therein, is properly to be considered the primary source for the institution of the *Shema*. The *Midrash Rabbah* on *Deuteronomy* (see the beginning of this note) has Moses himself interpolating (albeit in an undertone) the words "blessed be the name," etc. Maimonides could equally well have adduced this midrashic source, but in his halakhic code he prefers talmudic evidence.

[9]The omission of the particle *et* in no way militates against construing the second part of the verse as an object, and consequently in the accusative. First, biblical Hebrew evinces a mass of examples of accusatives (including objects governed by the verb *shama*, *hear*) without *et*, e.g., *1 Kings* 22:19; *Amos* 7:16; *Psalms* 17:6; 27:7; 28:2; 54:4; 143:1, etc. But quite apart from that, it is conceivable that the particle *et* is here deliberately omitted in order to circumvent any anthropomorphic interpretation. According to W. Gesenius (*Hebrew Grammar*, ed. E. Kautzsch, A.E. Cowley, 1910, section 117a-b), *et* essentially confers on the following accusative an immediacy of indication that an object-subject relationship exists, and it would therefore not be appropriate here. Israel was not intended to hear God's voice and thereby come to identify Him but through the voice, i.e., through the fact of hearing, were to become aware, through experience, of the existence of their God (*Deuteronomy* 4:12). Consequently the omission of *et* tends to tone down the object-reference of the accusative.

[10]*Ethics of the Fathers*, 6:2. (*Midrash Tanhuma* on *Exodus* 32:16, *Midrash Rabbah*, *Exodus* 41:7). For *bat kol* as there used ("daughter of a voice") in the sense of reverberations of the heavenly voice of God, see Babylonian Talmud, *Sanhedrin* 11a, *Tosafot*.

[11]Possibly one may translate in the same sense as Joshua ben Levi's adage a text which has occasioned no little difficulty to the scriptural commentators. *Deuteronomy* 5:19 (...*kol gadol ve-lo yasaf*) ought not to be rendered, as it usually is, "these words the Lord spoke...with a great voice, and added no more" (so King James' version); nor, as S.R. Hirsch has it, "spoke unto all your assembly...a mighty voice, and reached no further." *On the contrary*, one should rather translate "a great voice, *and did not cease*" (cf. Mishnah, *Ethics of the Fathers* 1:13, Hillel: *de-la mosif yasef.* "These

words the Lord spoke unto all your assembly in the mount out of the midst of the fire, of the cloud, and of the thick darkness, with a great voice that did not cease, i.e., the divine voice reverberates long after it sounded forth, and into perpetuity. This interpretation gains support from the *Targum Onkelos*, which renders the crucial words *ve-la pesak*, "and did not break off" (cease), even though Rashi construes the *Targum* as meaning "without intermission." Comp. Mecklenburg, *Ha-Ketav ve-ha-Kabbalah*, who unlike Rashi and most exegetes, translates it as "an unending voice." Hirsch's rendering is not satisfactory, since the voice was not limited, as he alleges, to a Jewish audience, but diffused itself through the entire world; cf. Babylonian Talmud, *Zevahim* 116a, *Midrash Exodus Rabbah* 5:9, etc. Nor can it be maintained that *ve-lo yasaf* means that Israel heard the first two commandments only from God Himself (cf. Babylonian Talmud, *Makkot* 23b and 24a), since that contention is refuted by the beginning of the verse, "these words the Lord spoke...;" cf. also Babylonian Talmud, *Shabbat* 88b.

[12]*Exodus* 24:7. Babylonian Talmud, *Shabbat* 88a emphasizes the significance of the word order: Israel undertakes to do whatever they are bidden, before they have even heard what it is.

[13]Also verse 15 and 19:19. On the occasion of the Sinaitic revelation, God permitted Moses' voice to be heard with the same timbre as his own, in order that Israel might still find it possible to hear God speaking to them in the subsequently promulgated detail which, at their own request (*Deuteronomy* 5:24), they heard from Moses.

[14]Rabbi David ben Joseph Abudraham, ad loc.; *Keli Yakar*, ad loc.

[15]Babylonian Talmud, *Berakhot* 13a-b, 14b; Maimonides, *Hilkhot Keriyat Shema* 2:1, *Shulhan Arukh, Orah Hayyim* 60:5. The precept of reciting the *Shema* is thus placed in a class above all the other commandments.

[16]See above, note 7.

CHAPTER IV

LIFE AS AN ORIGINAL BLESSING

I.   Introduction

The Talmud (*Hagigah* 14b) cautions students and scholars alike from exploring certain topics that defy empirical validation, verifiability or conceptual resolution. This cautionary statement, however, also serves as an appealing invitation to explore those topics. The interrelationship between psychology and religion reflects the ambivalence of the Talmudic story. It is precisely this ambivalence that requires further elucidation. Are psychology and religion mutually exclusive or complementary? Furthermore, historically and sociologically, the *average* religious person is not psychologically sophisticated and does not even appreciate the tremendous contribution that psychology has made to the welfare of humanity in the last century. Similarly, scholarly literature on the interrelationship of psychology and religion is scant. Carl Gustav Jung, William James, Gordon Allport and a few other writers are the notable exceptions. Sigmund Freud is generally interpreted as having substituted psychoanalysis for religion. Peter Gay (1987) even entitled his recent book on Freud *The Godless Jew*. This view, however, need not be the exclusive interpretation of Sigmund Freud's thoughts.

What exactly is the common fear in integrating psychology and religion? The average religious person understands religion to be ultimately based on faith in God, and trust in God who is omnipotent and omniscient. Doubts and deviations from normative practice seemingly represent a violation of the basic tenets of any religion. Changes in religious development in a life span are not openly encouraged, despite the universality of this phenomenon.

The typical believer usually divides life into at least two dichotomous parts. One part is the religious life, which requires unfailing obedience to a divine revelation and to a continuous ancestral tradition. The other part of life, that is either completely internalized or revealed exclusively in psychotherapy, consists of gnawing doubts and behavioral changes that are common to virtually everyone. This split, in and of itself, may produce an interminable guilt, with both psychological and bodily symptoms.

An educated guess is that the majority of religious people live with that split. They usually state that illness is illness and not related to any internal split within the psyche. The emotional guilt based on cognitive doubts is usually considered a normal part of life, and certainly, of religious life. Frequently, the average religious person associates illness with a previous theoretical or actual act of commission or omission that was contrary to religious belief and religious life. This Cartesian dualism of body and mind has also been expressed as the duality of body and soul. In contradistinction, the common denominator between religion and psychology is the striving for a complete unity and compatibility of body and soul.

Psychology strives primarily to understand the hidden aspect of each individual and relate it to the manifest aspect. The "external" frequently takes the form of behavior, communication and the projected image that one wants to share with others through clothing, general appearance and other mannerisms. The "internal" is the underlying processes of the behavior, and the metacommunication of communication. Simply stated, psychology strives for congruence between the conscious and the unconscious.

Religion is also represented by both external manifestations and an internal essence which is reflected in the worship of a Divine Being. Here as well, congruence is needed between conscious behavior and thoughts and the ever-expanding development of the soul.

Both psychology and religion represent the congruence of conscious and unconscious, or of the conscious and the soul. This unity is also the central motif of the holiest day in the Jewish calendar year, *Yom Kippur*, the Day of Atonement, which can also be written and understood as AT-ONE-MENT. On that holiest day, the goal that is set forth for each individual is to achieve a unity between the conscious and the unconscious in all different realms. Physicality and spirituality, action and reflection, attentiveness to divinity and focus on humanity -- all are subsumed under the category of the conscious and unconscious dichotomy.

Conscious and unconscious are complementary systems that can produce an ongoing homeostasis within each individual. This homeostasis constantly requires adjustment from conscious to unconscious, and from unconscious to conscious. It is a dynamic system.

On Becoming a Partner with God

In order to analyze this theory, I would like to demonstrate an aspect of psychological individuation, whereby an individual develops essential dimensions of the inner self. An important aspect of development in life is continued religious and psychological growth.

With this approach, the similarity between religion and psychology lies in the connection between the unconscious and the soul. According to Jung, the "unconscious" refers to the unknown of the inner world, "... everything which, involuntarily, and without paying attention to it, I feel, think, remember, want, and do ..." (Jung, *CW* 8, p. 185). The "soul" refers to "the depth of our psychic nature, and it contains in itself the faculty of relation to God" (Jung, *CW* 4, pp. 331 f.). The unconscious, like the soul, is the experience of divinity. Certainly, divinity is not limited to one's experience of divinity, but metaphysical issues and the essential nature of God are matters that philosophers and theologians can explore. The unconscious or soul is referred to as the God-aspect of the human and is called, in Biblical language, the "image of God" (Genesis 1:27).

This image of God is certainly not visible to the naked eye. It cannot be found in the body of human beings. It is not an organ, such as the brain, pancreas, liver or heart. Despite the lack of corporeality, this image is the most visible invisibility, precisely because it is the quintessential aspect of what makes a person "human." The more that the potential of the soul or the unconscious or the image of God becomes actualized, the more human each individual becomes. The more "human" each individual becomes, the more "Godlike" he or she becomes as well. What is significant is the realization that in the creation process, God created humanity with a potential to be as Godlike as humanly possible.

This approach differs qualitatively from the rather popular approach of striving to find meaning in life. Viktor Frankl (1984), the founder of logotherapy, emphasizes that each individual must find meaning in life.

This meaning is usually found in providing some human service to one's fellow and to society. In this way, one has participated in and contributed to *Tikkun ha-Olam*, a continuous maintenance and improvement of God's world and God's creations. In this way one becomes, metaphorically speaking, a partner with God. To qualitatively improve the world and to become a partner with God becomes a meaning of life. This type of meaning naturally applies to situations where suffering exists, on a personal or collective basis, or where suffering is potentially averted by maintaining the status quo and the many opportunities that are available to everyone.

Throughout life, the meaning and purpose of life, and the search for meaning in life constantly change depending on the situation. When one incorporates this attitude, tremendous objectives can be accomplished, both on an individual and a collective level.

A person who can make food more easily accessible, a person who can provide healing to others, a person who can facilitate education and security and a host of other purposeful and helpful objectives, has participated and contributed to *Tikkun ha-Olam*, the betterment of God's world.

Tikkun ha-Olam does not refer exclusively to the situation of others. It can also apply to the maintenance and welfare of one's own life. Trying to maintain one's emotional and physical health, providing adequate shelter and food, adapting to one's aging process, coping with the unexpected, and creating a social milieu, are all engaging goals, objectives and purposes of life.

This *Tikkun ha-Olam*, whether directed to oneself or others, also includes observing religious rituals. Prayers in synagogue, the practice of Jewish law and the study of Torah, are essential aspects that are included in *Tikkun ha-Olam*.

This concept has been beautifully summarized by Rabbi Elijah ben Solomon Zalman, more popularly known as the Vilna Gaon. He suggests that a person's religious life, or life in general, can be divided into one's relationship with God, one's relationship with people and one's relationship with oneself (Deuteronomy 32). The trinity of taking care of oneself, relating ethically to others and worshipping God encompasses all of *Tikkun ha-Olam*.

Soul Consciousness

An alternative approach, which may be superimposed upon *Tikkun ha-Olam*, can be referred to as the *human experience of Godlike qualities* in the psyche, conscious and unconscious.

What soul consciousness adds to *Tikkun ha-Olam* is the unique awareness and special feeling of the moment, in the here-and-now within oneself, that transforms that moment into eternity. Perhaps this concept is what William Blake referred to in his classic poem, "Auguries of Innocence" (1966):

> To see a world in a grain of sand,
> And a heaven in a wild flower,
> Hold infinity in the palm of your hand,
> And eternity in an hour.

This vision, this ability to see beyond the physical reality, and to experience the unseen presence of God in the ordinary, enables everyone to be in touch with Godlike attributes and to experience the *numinous*, the God within each one of us.

A new understanding emerges which conceptualizes each individual person as an *Olam Katan* (Israeli, 10th century), a microcosm of the entire universe. Each individual cannot only humanly experience love, hatred, fear, security, happiness, sadness, femininity, masculinity and all other emotions and feelings of life, but at the same time can realize that these characteristics and attributes also emanate from "the image of God," the soul," "the psyche," "the unconscious," i.e., that which constitutes a divine-human creation. This understanding ultimately leads to a leap into cosmic unity with God, and with all peoples and all cultures. The loneliness of each individual in the cosmos, throughout life and particularly at moments of crisis, serves as the stepping-stone to new concepts of reality, called "union with God."

A *Halakhic* (Jewish law) correlate, that each individual represents a microcosm, is found in the statement (Mishnah, *Sanhedrin* 4:5) that "one who saves a soul (person) is perceived as if one has sustained an entire universe." Each individual is compared to an entire world.

This microcosmic approach, which leads directly to a unifying framework with all people and cultures, diminishes and ultimately eliminates the intra-Jewish and inter-religious *polarization* which currently has resulted in cataclysmic dimensions of absurdity and a proportionate diminution of the "image of God" within each individual.

Two anecdotes illustrate how this polarization is counterproductive to any religious endeavor, worship of God or human fellowship. I visited and observed my Catholic brothers and sisters for a Good Friday religious service. I was appalled at the outright public declaration of anti-Semitism which was included in the liturgy from the Gospel of John (John 18 and 19). Particularly painful was the juxtaposition of the religious service with my generally very cordial and friendly relationship with many Catholics. How could the human psyche pray to God, yet denounce others at the same time? Even more blatant was the fact that many of the same nurses and physicians who attended religious services chastising the Jewish people would shortly thereafter prepare an intravenous solution for a Jewish patient or perform surgery on a Jewish patient. Furthermore, the same devout Catholics who prayed for the curse of the Jewish people would have lunch with me or at other times seek my professional advice as a psychologist. The universal Catholic liturgy is still focused on the primitive religious concept of "us and them," the in-group and the out-group dichotomy.

The day after Good Friday happened to be Passover (frequently both holidays coincide). I attended a synagogue for the Passover services, hoping to hear the central message of the Passover holiday: to develop sensitivity for the suffering of other people, thereby bringing closer the ultimate redemption of all people. I was not only disappointed, but actually devastated. The Rabbi's sermon advocated the condemnation of Christians for their historical blood libel accusation directed at the Jewish people. Here it was, all in the name and worship of God: Catholics condemn the Jewish people in their Good Friday service, and Jews reciprocate with their condemnation of Catholics on the Passover Festival. Negative judgment is rampant. The unconscious, the psyche, the soul is entirely absent. Even "consciousness" is hard to find in either religious group. (In subsequent years, the offensive Catholic liturgy was altered due to my intervention. The leadership of both the Church and Synagogue expressed appreciation for my thoughts.)

This general lack of ecumenical respect and understanding is equally pervasive within the different denominations of the Jewish people. *Hasidic*, Orthodox, Conservative, Reform, Reconstructionist, secular, atheist, humanistic and agnostic Jews rarely cooperate or demonstrate genuine respect and empathy for one another. Fortunately, within each one of the movements there have been and still are a few Rabbinic and lay leaders who see and function beyond their territory and provincialism. But for the most part, the tolerance for divergent views is nearly extinct. Here again, the in-group philosophy becomes sanctified. Denominations frequently foster similar dress and physical appearance, a rather well-defined and narrow ideology and a holier-than-thou attitude.

Group Narcissism

The aforementioned attitude or dichotomy is similar to Fromm's concept of group narcissism (1973), which he views as one of the most important sources of human aggression. Group narcissism is a *pathological* manifestation on the collective basis of an individual's narcissistic personality. A narcissistic personality experiences:

> his body, his needs, his feelings, his thoughts, his property, everything and everybody pertaining to him as fully real, while everybody and everything that does not form part of the person or is not an object of his needs is not interesting, is not fully real, is perceived only by intellectual recognition, while affectively without weight and color. A person, to the extent to which he is narcissistic, has a double standard of perceptions. Only he himself and what pertains to him has significance, while the rest of the world is more or less weightless or colorless, and because of this double standard the narcissistic person shows severe defects in judgment and lacks the capacity for objectivity. (Fromm, 1973, p. 201)

In group narcissism, the object is not the individual, but the group to which one belongs. Group narcissism asserts that "either my country or my religion is the most wonderful, the most cultured, the most powerful and the most peace-loving" (Fromm, 1973, p 202). These attitudes sound like an expression of patriotism, faith and loyalty. This approach is shared by many members of the same group, and the resulting consensus creates a form of reality for most of the people of that nation or religion.

Group narcissism has significant sociological functions. It enhances the solidarity and cohesion of the group. It gives satisfaction to the members of the group. Even an individual who usually feels miserable may frequently compensate by feeling a part of "the most wonderful group in the world." Indeed, one's degree of group narcissism is commensurate with the lack of real satisfaction in one's life. The ideology of group narcissism ostensibly defends human dignity, decency, morality and right. Devilish qualities are ascribed to the other group; it is treacherous, ruthless, cruel and basically inhuman. When group narcissism is inflicted with a wound, real or imaginary, the reaction is very intense, leading to hostility.

In contradistinction to the in-group/out-group dichotomy, in which one group constantly decries and chastises the other, is the microcosmic approach, in which different cultures and differences among people can be appreciated and ultimately seen as mutually enhancing. Differences between peoples can be seen as the various symbols people have developed in order to cope and to probe the mysteries of the world and of life.

Holiness and Eating

This theory can be illustrated with a very basic example: the different rituals surrounding eating, food and family meals. In Judaism, tremendous emphasis is placed on the observance of the dietary laws. There is a prohibition against eating dairy products together with meat (Exodus 23:19 and 34:26; Deuteronomy 14:21). Animals meeting certain specific criteria are deemed fit for consumption, while others are prohibited. All cultures have special foods that are often associated with different festivals. Some cultures eat while reclining, or in other positions, while others use special utensils, depending on the food or the occasion. Different cultures have varying rituals before, during and after eating. Why are there so many differences surrounding eating, particularly since eating is one of the most basic and necessary activities to maintain life?

I suggest that there is a universal reason for the mystery surrounding the consumption of food. In order to maintain life, we must destroy life. If we consume meat, an animal life is destroyed. If we consume fruit, although the tree bears more fruit, tree life has been detached. If we consume vegetables, although plant life is perennial, an aspect of plant life has been destroyed. The maintenance of our life necessitates the destruction of other forms of life. Granted there is a qualitative difference between human life, animal life and plant life, but nevertheless, other forms of life need to be destroyed before we are able to maintain our basic biological need of nourishing our bodies. That is why different cultures have developed various symbols and rituals for the eating process. In Judaism, although no explicit reason is suggested for the underlying motif of observing the dietary laws (which are considered *Hok*, statutory law), the end result of observing dietary laws is described as the process of achieving holiness, *Kedushah* (Leviticus 11:44). The Hebrew word *Kedushah* is a very difficult word to translate adequately. Some translate it as "holiness," while others translate it as "separateness." "Separateness" refers to the fact that some potentially tasty foods are not permitted. Thus, the food that is allowed is "separate" from the prohibited food. This word *Kedushah* (holiness or separateness) is the Hebrew word for Rudolph Otto's concept, expressed by the word *numinosity* (Otto, 1923).

A *numinous* feeling is the human experience that is ultimately ineffable, the unique transcendental experience of the tremendous mystery of God, our relationship to God, and to life itself. The otherwise demonic act of destroying life to sustain life is transformed through the symbolism and ritual of the dietary laws to an experience of *Kedushah*, holiness, an experience of the *numinous*. This experience is, of necessity, universal, because all people, all cultures, all races destroy life in order to sustain human life. Different religions are encouraged to maintain certain specific rituals and cultures and at the same time, realize the importance of the symbols of other religions. Thus, the dietary laws are ultimately designed to emphasize the universality of humanity, while respecting the specific differences of each culture. Unfortunately, these same laws have not only created unhealthy separateness between Jew and Jew; but also, within each sectarian movement, observance of the dietary laws has brought untold anguish and misery to family life and community life, as more and more people are choosing to eat with fewer and fewer people. The observance of the dietary laws needs to be complemented by an awareness of their underlying *Kedushah.*

Symbols

Psychology and religion, as mutually-enhancing fields of study and ways of life, can restore the beautiful and original meanings to the symbols of all religions. Over the course of history, the essence of symbols may become distorted and, indeed, antithetical to their original meaning. There has developed a diminution of the "image of God," "the soul," "the unconscious" and "the psyche." When the communal and individual soul dies, the divine-human is transformed into a demon-human, for whom religious law and practice become dry ends without purpose. Ritualistic differences become sacrosanct. Human insecurities are transformed into negative, projected judgments. Geographical territories become the *raison d'etre* for wars. Rites of passage become rites and not passages. Death becomes an enemy and not a natural development of life. Synagogues, temples and churches become vehicles for ego-fulfillment, and the poet dies.

The original intent of symbols, however, can restore the divine-human image and heighten the mystery of life and the experience of the *numinous* within each and every individual. Religious law then becomes a natural part of life, as the conscious and the unconscious are awakened and reawakened to life. The manifestation of religious law represents the twin images of the essence of the behavior and the soul of the individual. Universals can become common. Black, white, brown and yellow can primarily represent colors and secondarily, shades of differences. The Passover *Seder* celebration can be the stimulus for a heightened sensitivity to suffering in any part of the world. Negative judgment of others may become internalized as a reflection of some internal dissonance in each individual. The typology of the arch-enemy Esau can be understood as an Esau within the Jacob.

All land can potentially become sacred: Canada, the Soviet Union, Australia, Israel or Egypt. It can be sanctified by the human soul particular to each country. Rites of passage can emphasize psychological, social and spiritual passage, as when a young boy becomes a *Bar-Mitzvah* and a young girl becomes a *Bat-Mitzvah.* Death can be seen as a friend that ultimately releases every individual from temporary eternity to eternal eternity. Houses of prayer can each become a *Mikdash Me'at*, a miniature Holy of Holies. The voice of Isaiah (56:7) proclaims: "Even these will I bring to my holy mountain, and make them joyful in my house of prayer; their burnt-offerings and their sacrifices shall be accepted upon my altar; *for my house shall be called a house of prayer for all the nations.*"

The poet, artist, singer, musician, writer and dreamer within each and every individual can be resurrected. The person who has writer's block can be transformed into a prolific writer, and the person who has never remembered a dream can become a contemporary Joseph.

The Natural Person

The spirit and power of the human soul has been *Halakhically* codified in the liturgy of the three main festivals: Pesach, Shavuot and Sukkot. The Talmud states (*Betzah* 17a) that when a festival and a Sabbath coincide, the text of one blessing is: "Who sanctifies the Sabbath, *Israel*, and sanctifies the appointed seasons." The weekly Sabbath is divinely sanctified from the time of the six days of creation. The festivals, however, are determined each time by the power and spirit of the Jewish courts to declare the exact time and date of a new moon, thereby determining the dates and the holidays as well. This process explains the juxtaposition of the word "Israel" that occurs *after* the word Sabbath, but *before* the words "appointed seasons." The power of the human spirit has many ramifications and implications.

Sanctity is not a concept external to individuals. Individuals often determine sanctity. Sanctity may take the singular form of imbuing a natural panoramic view with a person's feeling of awe and majesty. Or, it may be a very special moment of two individuals meeting one another on a very deep psychological level. Or, it may be when a person relates to the Self, not in relationship to any external aspect of nature, nor in relationship to another person. These moments can be transformed into peak experiences of sanctity. The naturalness of each individual's existence and self-reflection can bring and create Divine consciousness.

Psychology as the handmaiden of religion, and religion as the handmaiden of psychology will not create the *Halakhic Man* (Soloveitchik, 1944), or the *Psycho-Halakhic Man of Conscience* (Meier, 1986). Rather, these circumstances can produce a natural person, whose religion, with all of its components, will be a natural function. This natural religious function, understood properly, can include conscious and unconscious processes.

As Moses' face was radiant through his contact with the *Shekhinah* (Divine Presence), so will the "image of God" within each individual radiate to all the environment. People will proclaim, "This is a Godly person" and emulate the exemplary model. The *Koran Or Panav* (light beamed from his face) referring to Moses is not to be understood to mean horns, as Michelangelo understood Scripture (Exodus 34:29), but rather as an eternal light, whose rays extend and illustrate the entire world. The eternal light which is found in every synagogue in front of the Holy Ark (*Aron ha-Kodesh*) will pale in contrast to the living eternal light. This eternal light can serve as a beam of light, as a natural guide and counselor. It can provide the necessary warmth to create the ambience necessary for love, life, intimacy and procreation, where life begets life, and a new divine-child is born.

The birth of a divine-child is described in the Talmud as emanating from a father, a mother and God. The Talmud states (*Niddah* 31b) that "there are three partners in the birth and creation of each individual: God, a father and a mother." While the father and mother provide the physical features, their sexual union provides the divine soul. This beautiful religious statement allows one to speculate on the most profound psychological meaning of life.

Adam, the first individual created by God, is described as initially being both male and female (Genesis 1:27). This Adam represents the archetype of all future men and women. *Each* man and *each* woman contains both the archetype male and the archetype female, despite being biologically only of a single sex.

What is the nature of a male who has both a male archetype and a female archetype? And, what is the nature of a female who has both a female archetype and a male archetype? Women and men have certain psychological and physical characteristics that are similar, yet other emotional and anatomical components differentiate them.

Contemporary Western society, like other cultures past and present, has rigidly adhered to specific sex roles, norms, expectations and social etiquette. When babies are born, males are wrapped in blue blankets and females are wrapped in pink blankets. When gifts are given for birthdays or other special occasions, toy fire engines are given to males and dolls are given to females. These and similar stereotypes continue throughout life. Tears are considered an appropriate response for a female under certain circumstances, yet an immature or inappropriate response for a male under similar circumstances.

Naturally, there are significant biological differences that have their psychological correlates. Nursing creates the natural situation in which the mother is initially the primary nutritional caretaker. This role frequently gives rise to a unique bonding between mother and child. The female menstrual cycle naturally creates more focus on and awareness of days, weeks, months and time in general. Indeed, it has been suggested by Norman Lamm (1966) that females are exempt from Biblical and Rabbinic commandments that are regulated by time precisely because of their intuitive awareness and sensitivity to their bodily clocks.

Other differences between the sexes concern age-related changes regarding reaction time for sexual desire, potency and relations. The gerontological literature (Birren and Schaie, 1977) is very detailed in this area.

Despite these significant biological and psychological differences throughout one's life span, the individual psyche of each male and female is identical to Adam's primordial soul, containing both anima (female) and animus (male).

Sexuality and Spirituality

The anima and animus of each psyche, of each soul, of each unconscious, is naturally derived from one of the most intense spiritual, psychological, emotional and biological acts of which any human being is capable -- the sexual act. The sexual foreplay to sexual relations may frequently include a passionate kiss which symbolizes how two separate human beings share one breath for a short period of time. The mouth-to-mouth contact maintains two unique lives with one breath of life. Not only are two lives maintained momentarily, but each life sustains the other with a shared breath that goes back and forth. Such a relationship expresses itself and finds fulfillment in all dimensions: the biological desire, the psychological craving for intimacy, the emotional togetherness of two individuals, and a spiritual union where each partner gives "spirit" to the other.

The sexual act is the quintessential act of two human beings becoming a unified one. It is precisely at this moment that nakedness does not express shame, embarrassment or humiliation, but rather the potential for ultimate spiritual bliss of oneness and a return to primordial Adam. Primordial Adam represented male and female in one; sexual relations, likewise, represent a short time period when male and female are united physically, spiritually, psychologically and emotionally. It is precisely at that moment that a new soul, another individual created in the image of God, can be created. This new individual can be either a male or female human being, but its soul contains the male and female archetypes of the parents. This child and every child becomes a divine-child, created in the image of God.

The image of God is introduced to Moses as "I AM THAT I AM" (Exodus 3:14). This very complex appellation can be understood to indicate that the image of God changes, depending on the perception of each individual for each particular situation. At a time of war, the image of God may appear as a Mighty Warrior. At a time of famine, the image of God may manifest itself as Someone Who Sustains Everyone. The name of God that represents the all-abiding Presence is the feminine image of God, known as the Shekhinah. The image of God referred to as Shekhinah denotes the Presence of God to the heart, mind and soul that is open. The image of God contains the male and female, as well as the archetype primordial Adam. Each sexual union represents the male/female unity that gives birth to an image of its parents, similar to them, yet unique.

In the process of giving life, the male/female union becomes Divine-like and creative, just as God acted at the very beginning of the creation process. The birthing process for humans is lifelong and takes many different forms.

The words "IN THE BEGINNING" (Genesis 1:1) can apply throughout one's life. Each moment, each day, each week, each month, each holiday and each year can be a new beginning for creativity and a deepening of life's experiences. Relationships that have become dull and boring over the years can be transformed with "IN THE BEGINNING" -- by infusing "light," meaning new energy. Parent-child relationships can be transformed from knowing each other superficially to listening to each other's life journey with "IN THE BEGINNING" -- renewed creativity with new awakenings to be able to listen without being judgmental. Lifelong neuroses of depression and anxiety can be transformed into stepping-stones as one explores the unconscious. The image of God as a Lawgiver can be supplemented with the image of God as the Shekhinah, the all-embracing female Presence of God. Even at death one can say "IN THE BEGINNING," as death is transformed from a frightening event into a mystical union with God. The death of a righteous person is pictured in Rabbinic literature as a Divine kiss (Talmud, *Moed Katan* 28a). Just as a male/female kiss represents the sustaining of a shared life, so too God's "kiss" symbolically represents a mystical marriage between God and each individual at the moment of death.

Just as the birth of Adam is described as the blowing of a Divine breath into the nostrils (Genesis 2:7), this breath is retrieved at the end of life with a Divine kiss.

My analyst, James Kirsch, shared with me a recurring dream that had a bicycle in it. The two wheels represented religion and psychology. These two were really one -- the unconscious, individual and collective, representing the deepest layer in the psyche, the source of infinite Divine knowledge.

Anima and Animus

The union of the anima and animus has both an external and an internal representation. The external form is the sacred union of marriage which commences when the groom recites to his bride under the marriage canopy: "Behold, you are *sanctified* unto me through the giving of this ring to you according to the laws, mores and customs of Moses and Israel" (Talmud, *Kiddushin* 5b).

Once again, the theme of *Kedushah* relates to a very basic aspect of life, a sacred marriage. Here again, the two meanings of *Kedushah* are applicable. The *Kedushah*-"separate" notion refers to the legalistic aspect, i.e., that the sexual relationship of these two distinct and specific individuals, to the exclusion of anyone else, is legally sanctioned by religious law. Although other individuals may be physically, emotionally and spiritually desirable, sexual union with them is prohibited under religious law. The *Kedushah*-"holiness" notion refers to the sacred union of male and female on a spiritual level, where the male's anima is projected onto his selected spouse, and the female's animus is projected onto her selected spouse, thereby creating a new unity. This new anima-animus union is a recreation of primordial Adam, who was created as male and female in one.

Ultimately, however, one strives for an anima-animus marriage within oneself. On spiritual, psychological and emotional dimensions, a sacred marriage takes place. Each individual is created with *pairs* of organs and limbs. The eyes represent a visual marriage; the ears, an auditory union. The right hand clasps the left hand in physical unity; similarly, the right hemisphere of the brain and the left hemisphere represent systems that are complementary. These unions, marriages, complementary systems and physical unities all come together in the sanctity of one whole soul.

Life as an Original Blessing

Success in marriage is not only finding the right partner, but becoming the right person, allowing the natural processes to evolve. In Western civilization, Christians are imbued with original sin. However, a contemporary Catholic theologian has suggested an alternative concept - original blessing (Fox, 1983).

How is it possible to live life as an original blessing, and what indeed does this phrase mean? Original blessing acknowledges human life as the supreme Divine gift. Original blessing allows for constant human creativity and renewed spirituality throughout life. It is based on a heart that is open to the beauty of the world and the uniqueness of each individual. Original blessing confers blessings throughout life. It refers to the lifelong creative process of seeking to discover the renewed meanings and experiences of life. Original blessing can allow the individual to achieve harmony within the self. When harmony within the self is achieved, it facilitates the process of developing harmony within the universe and intimate harmony with another person. Harmony is frequently the result of an ongoing creative process, whereby a new unity is discovered among concepts which had heretofore been disparate and disjointed. These insights may be precipitated by an experience of nature, an appreciation of art, religious experiences, scientific discoveries and other ecstatic experiences. These experiences that lead to a new wholeness and union with the universe are frequently accompanied by overwhelming feelings. This process allows each individual to discover and express his or her own uniqueness. The inner marriage and special union with oneself and the universe can take place when individuals are true to themselves and have followed the path which nature intended them to follow. Scrupulous attention to the inner voice of the psyche -- which manifests itself in dreams, fantasies and other derivatives of the unconscious -- assists the soul on its path.

This path of self-development is called the process of individuation. This process, which aims toward "wholeness" or "integration," is one in which the different elements of the psyche, both conscious and unconscious, form a new unity.

This new integration is essentially an internal matter, a change in attitude taking place within the psyche of the individual. This process brings an inner peace of mind. This process is not healing through insight, nor through making a new and better relationship with another person, nor even through solving particular problems, but healing by means of an inner change of attitude. This sense of peace and acceptance of life, of being part of a greater whole, is the experience of a new unity within.

This process is not a static mental state which is maintained uninterrupted or forever. This development of the personality toward integration is always bound to be superseded.

The achievement of optimum development is a journey that is continuous throughout life. The path of individuation and the changes of attitude which take place are always accompanied by creative processes. New ideas arise, and inspiration occurs during both one's waking and sleeping hours. Ideas and images are allowed to appear and take their course spontaneously. This process represents overwhelming forces which happen within the mind. The creator is passive, while the creativity has a volition of its own. This creativity frequently forms new links between formerly disparate entities, a union of opposites. The manifest creative process continues throughout life, reflecting the process of individuation which takes place largely in solitude.

The human mind seems to be so constructed that the discovery, or perception, or order, or unity in the external world is mirrored, transformed and experienced as if it were a discovery of a new order and balance in the inner world of the psyche. Outer happenings and inner experiences interact with one another. Seeing the perfect balance of colors in a painting, or hearing the integration of opposing themes in a piece of music gives the observer or the listener the experience of a new unity, both without and within.

Similarly, the process of reducing inner discord and reaching a degree of unification with the psyche has a positive effect upon the subject's perception of, and relation with, the external world.

Implications for the Interrelationship of Psychology and Religion

The entity that psychology and religion have in common is the soul. Both analysts and clergy can share this common frontier as patients, clients and parishioners bare their souls. Each individual painfully shares his or her suffering and experience of life.   Both analysis and clinical pastoral counseling enhance meanings and transform life events into experiences, while creating a living religion.

James Hillman (1984) shares a beautiful story, the gist of which I have also experienced at Cedars-Sinai Medical Center. He says:

> I watched a women being interviewed. She sat in a wheelchair because she was elderly and feeble. She said that she was dead for she had lost her heart. The psychiatrist asked her to place her hand over her breast to feel her heart beating: it must still be there if she could feel its beat. "That," she said, "is not my real heart." She and the psychiatrist looked at each other. There is nothing more to say. Like the primitive who has lost his soul, she had lost the loving courageous connection to life -- and that is the real heart, not the

ticker which can well pulsate isolated in a glass bottle. (Hillman, 1984, p.43)

Both the rabbi and the psychologist strive to help the modern Jew search for a soul. The rabbi often emphasizes rituals, liturgy and synagogue activities.   However, this approach is inadequate.   Just as Adam was expelled by God from the Garden of Eden, the reverse has now taken place. Ironically, the living God has now been expelled from many synagogues, Jewish laws and rituals, and prayer.

Both psychology and religion, represented as a symbolic bicycle, must strive to facilitate each individual's experiences of the unconscious in order to find the soul. The unconscious is experiential, and it is derived from a living experience.   The living reality of the soul comes as an accidental happening. The Bible uses the expression *Mikreh* or *Hakreh* -- an accidental happening (Genesis 24:12; 44:29) -- to exemplify the reality of the experience of a living God.

Once this door is opened, another world is revealed. The ordinary takes on a new sense for oneself. Things that have been long forgotten return with new meanings. Childhood is revisited. This process may be understood by considering unexplored life as a sealed bottle of water, devoid of any source of new water. The water has become dusty and dirty. The pressure mounts. Pains, hurts and suffering remain constantly with us. The water remains stagnant and gives off an unpleasant odor. Finally, the rubber stopper or cork is removed as a revitalizing experience.

The stagnant water begins to flow, and the journey of life begins. Not the autobiographical journey of one's life. Not the information that is written on tombstones -- the dates of birth and death -- but the births and deaths of one's inner journey and experience of life and of God. Tragedies of life become the stepping-stones and opportunities for climbing Jacob's ladder of ascension. We come face to face with our entire Self, including the dark truths about ourselves. The experience of the inner darkness is the vivid confrontation with one's repressed nature. Ultimately, we realize that we alone are responsible for our character traits and who we are. Not our mother, not our father, not God, not our spouse and not our children -- but we, ourselves, climb the ladder or fall down or never begin the climb.

Initially, in therapeutic sessions, the focus is placed on how strange the events and people are in the circumstances of life in which the client is the center. As the sessions progress, the client realizes that life is ultimately the encounter with the self -- which becomes transformed in the encounter into the *Self* -- i.e., that which incorporates the image of God.

This same process takes place in a person's relationship to the image of God. Initially, one keeps a fixed image of God and suggests all types of cognitive casuistic reasoning to account for all of one's difficult experiences of life. But this approach is not consistent with the second of the Ten Words or Commandments (Exodus 20:4). One's image of God should not be graven or immutable. One should realize that the image of God constantly changes throughout one's lifetime. Towards the end of Job's life, he states, in essence, that throughout my life I have heard of God by hearsay, but now my eyes see You by my own life experience (Job 42:5).

"I am the Lord your God" (Exodus 20:2) refers to the image of God both as a Mighty Warrior and as an Elder who is full of compassion (*Midrash Rabbah*, Exodus 20:2). Ultimately, each of us encounters our Self as we ascend our own ladder. The image of God changes for each individual throughout life. When we arrive at the end of our lifetime, hopefully we will meet the Angel of Death as an angel, and we will have had a *fullness* of days as did Job. The angel will kiss each individual, and we will each die as Job died, being old and full of days (Job 42:17).

References

Altmann, Alexander and Stern, S.M. (Eds.) (1958). *Isaac Israeli: A neoplatonic philosopher of the early tenth century*. London: Oxford University Press.

Birren, J.E. and Schaie, K.W. (Eds.) (1977). *Handbook of the psychology of aging*. New York: Van Nostrand Reinhold.

Blake, W. (1966). *The complete writings of William Blake*, ed. by Geoffrey Keynes. Oxford: Oxford University Press.

Fox, M. (1983). Original blessing: *A primer in creation spirituality*. Santa Fe, New Mexico: Bear and Co.

Frankl, V. (1984). *Man's search for meaning: An introduction to logotherapy*. New York: Simon & Schuster.

Fromm, E. (1973). *The anatomy of human destructiveness*. New York: Holt, Rinehart and Winston.

Gay, P. (1987). *A godless Jew: Freud, atheism and the making of psychoanalysis*. New Haven and London: Yale University Press.

Hillman, J. (1984). *In search: Psychology and religion*. Dallas: Spring Publications, Inc.

The Holy Scriptures (1985). Philadelphia: Jewish Publication Society.

Jung, C.G. *Collected works*. (20 vols.) (1969). Princeton, N.J.: Princeton University Press.

Lamm, N. (1966). *A hedge of roses: Jewish insights into marriage and married life*. New York: Feldheim.

Meier, L. (1986). The psycho-*Halakhic* man of conscience. *Journal of Psychology and Judaism, 10*(2), 19-45.

Midrash. (10 vols.) (1961). H. Freedman and M. Simons (Eds.). London: Soncino Press.

New Testament (1970). *New American Bible.* New York: Catholic Book Publishing Co

Otto, R. (1967). *The idea of the holy.* New York: Oxford University Press. (Originally published 1923.)

Soloveitchik, J.B. (1983). *Halakhic man.* Translated by Lawrence Kaplan. Philadelphia: Jewish Publication Society. Originally published 1944.

The Talmud. (18 vols.) (1961). I. Epstein (Ed.). London: Soncino Press.

CHAPTER V

THE STAR OF DAVID AS A SYMBOL
OF THE UNION OF OPPOSITES

I. Introduction

Just as the sun rises in the east and sets in the west, so the shadow of each individual rises in the west and sets in the east. These similar but opposing directions of the light-dark dichotomy stand in stark contrast to the disproportionate size of the shadow in relation to each individual, as reflected in the morning and in the evening. Each person, indeed, casts a giant shadow. Interestingly, the shadow disappears entirely only when the sun is directly above the individual at midday, shining the brightest. This image of the natural sunshine and its corresponding shadow finds its counterpart in picturing the complexity of human nature and its two opposing tendencies, the *Yetzer ha-Tov* and the *Yetzer ha-Ra* (the good and evil tendencies).

A beautiful story relates how the duality of human nature is reflected in the symbols of light and darkness. For twelve years, Rabbi Simeon bar Yochai and his son were in a cave, studying and meditating about the secrets of the universe (Talmud, *Shabbat* 33b). After digesting all the intricacies of the world and of humanity, Rabbi Simeon bar Yochai felt prepared and ready to reenter the world and relate to family, friends and environment. As he and his son exited the cave, the brightness of the light of the world was overwhelming, and "whatever they looked upon was immediately burned." After an additional twelve months of exploration, they exited for a second time, this time, however, with a successful adaptation to and integration in the world.

The wisdom of this story is in its description of the brightness of pure spirituality as blinding light. Light is a metaphor that conveys the uniqueness of each individual through the journey of life. Although light is obviously necessary as a guide for life, too much light creates blindness.

Blinding light represents a state of human purity that is unachievable. This is the same blinding light of midday, when the human shadow is totally eclipsed. When Rabbi Simeon bar Yochai initially exited, his understanding was Platonic and idealistic, not realistic. It was pure light, excluding the indigenous darkness that coexists with light

In the creation story, darkness precedes the creation of light, and light is God's first creation (Genesis 1:2, 3). The first act of God was the creation of light by the utterance of "Let there be light" (Genesis 1:3). However, light could only be created if darkness preceded it. There was darkness before creation -- coexisting with the infinite God.

Darkness and light, *Yetzer ha-Ra* and *Yetzer ha-Tov*, exist as polarities both in the physical world and in the creation of humanity. Just as light can only emerge from darkness, so also the *Yetzer ha-Tov* can only be recognized when one is always cognizant of the eternal existence of the *Yetzer ha-Ra*.

Darkness

What do the darkness and shadow of human nature mean and how are they manifest? They have been and continue to be reflected in the universal history of humanity, the national history of each nation, the particular religion of each ethnic group, the family unit and quintessentially, within each individual.

Biblical writings, particularly the early Prophetic works, are replete with accounts of wars and violence, to such an extent that only a few times during Biblical history does the text recount that there was tranquility and peace for forty years (Judges 3:11, 5:31 and 8:28) and only once for eighty years (Judges 3:30). The histories of many individual nations reflect civil wars, the triumph of Machiavellian power struggles, and social upheavals surrounding contemporary social issues, such as those we face now in the United States of America. From Islam to Christianity to Judaism, each religious group has been responsible, in varying degrees, for a lack of tolerance of others. Communism, a political system that denies the validity of any organized religion, represents the oppressive society par excellence. The collective destructiveness of nations, religions and ethnicities is based on the destructive tendencies of the individuals who form the various collectives.

The darkness and shadow of humanity seemed even to exceed the parameters anticipated by God (Genesis 6:6, "And God repented having made humanity on the earth, and He grieved"). At one point, in the very early period of Biblical history, God expresses regret for having created humanity, since all the self-created thoughts and behaviors of people have been and continue to be evil (Hirsch, Genesis 6:5). After the Flood, God expresses the thought that the *collective whole* will never again be exterminated due to the new realization that the thoughts of individuals are evil from the very beginning of their childhood (Genesis 8:21). Despite the Creator's realization that each individual is created with the potential for good and evil (Genesis 2:7 and Talmud *Berakhot* 61a), the actuality and the execution of extreme and intense evil seemed to surprise even God.

The reverse has also been experienced. The mysteriousness and impenetrable essence of the changing images of God have perplexed and surprised the Jewish people and humanity as a whole. How could the image of God, as presented to Abraham, even contemplate testing Abraham's faith by asking him to sacrifice his son Isaac (Genesis 22:1)? Is this not the epitome of an evil request? In contemporary terms, how could the image of God as presented to the European Jewish community of the 1930's and 1940's, test the contemporary Abrahams, Isaacs, Jacobs, Sarahs, Rebeccahs, Rachels, and Leahs, their children and their parents during the *Shoah* (the European destruction carried out by Germany's Third Reich)? How could a God silently observe the perpetration of these unimaginable atrocities carried out on a people, "chosen" or not? The evil image of such a silent God is certainly mysterious and staggering.

If Abraham, our Patriarch, presented himself to the Cedars-Sinai Medical Center's emergency room for voluntary psychiatric help in assisting him to decide whether or not to obey God's command, as he heard it, to sacrifice his son to God, what type of assistance would he receive? Despite the inappropriateness of superimposing a twentieth-century milieu on a Biblical event that occurred approximately nineteen centuries B.C.E., there is no doubt in my mind that Abraham, our Patriarch, would be put on a 72-hour psychiatric hold as an inpatient in the hospital's Mental Health Unit, with a diagnosis of an acute psychotic breakdown, based on auditory hallucinations that could lead to his son's murder.

What emerges from this discussion is God's response to the darkness and shadow of humanity and humanity's surprise at the darkness and shadow of God. The following discussion reflects the *human psyche's* struggle as it strives to explore the mysteries and experiences of life.

This darkness of God coexisted with the spirit of God (Genesis 1:2) and preceded any part of creation, even light. Thus, what is being suggested is that the image of God that is in every person (Genesis 1:26) is the same aspect of the image of God that exists for God. The diametrically opposed tendencies of good and evil exist in humanity specifically because they exist in God, the Creator. Humanity is like the image of God, and the image of God is similar to the image of humanity.

This concept of darkness and shadow as a part of the image of God is homiletically discovered by analyzing the Hebrew word for the image of God, *Tzelem.* The root of *Tzelem* is *Tzel,* which means shadow. The image of God includes the shadow, and it is precisely this dichotomous nature of God that determines the uniqueness of God and humanity.

Union of Opposites

Epistemologically, the perceived nature of reality is the union of opposites. There is light and there is darkness. There is beauty and there is ugliness. There is wisdom and there is ignorance. This perceived nature of reality, must of necessity apply to the perceived nature of the essential image of God. Humanity has no other experiential or epistemological basis but to try to fathom the image of God with the same concepts by which it understands natural reality.

What does the union of opposites mean? This phrase refers to a bipolar, never-ending continuum, that can be illustrated as follows:

infinity<--bad	-5 -4 -3 -2 -1 • 1 2 3 4 5	good------->infinity
infinity<--dark	-5 -4 -3 -2 -1 • 1 2 3 4 5	light------->infinity
infinity<--selfish	-5 -4 -3 -2 -1 • 1 2 3 4 5	altruistic-->infinity
infinity<--ill	-5 -4 -3 -2 -1 • 1 2 3 4 5	healthy---->infinity
infinity<--ugly	-5 -4 -3 -2 -1 • 1 2 3 4 5	beautiful-->infinity

The essence of creation is the creation of bipolar infinite continua. This understanding explains why light was created first. It served as the complementary bipolar infinite continuum to the pre-existing "darkness." The union of opposites refers to the creation of a unit or a unity. There could be good precisely because bad also existed. There could be light precisely because there was dark.

Before creation, when darkness coexisted with God, the state of the world was *Tohu va-Vohu* (Genesis 1:2), a state of utter void, chaos and total confusion. No opposites existed and therefore nothing could be apprehended.

The Star of David

This union of opposites, reflecting the essence of God, humanity and creation, has been symbolically expressed by the Star of David, one of the most significant symbols in Judaism. The Star of David is portrayed as follows:

The Star of David is represented as two interlocking triangles, one pointing upwards and one pointing downwards. These opposing directions represent the eternal struggle and tension between the dark and shadow side, and the light and bright side of each individual. The Star of David has always appeared to me with the addition of a dot in the center, as follows:

That dot, represented as equidistant from the top and bottom points of the two triangles, reflects the position of each individual in relation to the two ways that are open to that person in the journey of life.

Human Nature

The essence of human nature is the realization of its *dual* aspect, a composite of diametrically opposed tendencies of good and evil. Philosophical systems throughout the ages have debated the issue of whether human nature is basically evil or basically good. Strong arguments have been expressed in support of both views. This chapter suggests that human nature is neither good nor bad, but potentially both. The only statement that can be made is that *human nature exists.* If the thoughts and behaviors are good, we can say retrospectively that human nature manifests itself in a positive manner. If the thoughts and behaviors are bad, we can say retrospectively that human nature manifests itself in a negative manner.

The two strong negative statements in Genesis (6:5 and 8:21) are not statements about human nature in general, but rather descriptive statements based on the two preceding historical accounts of evil, the first concerning perverted sexuality, and the second describing the generation of Noah and the Flood.

This duality of human nature is well documented by the Biblical description of the lives of our patriarchs and matriarchs. Never are their shortcomings and deficiencies omitted or overlooked. Conversely, with regard to the archenemy, Esau, his virtues of filial devotion are accentuated (Genesis 27:41).

This duality of human nature is similarly explained by the phrases *Yetzer ha-Tov* and *Yetzer ha-Ra*, the good and evil potentialities of individuals. Both phrases refer to *future* behaviors of individuals (Hirsch, Genesis 6:5), that is, what will take place. That is the mystery of everyone's life journey. Some journeys are initially composed of continuous evil behavior and then are gradually transformed into continuous good behavior. For others, the reverse takes place. For most people, however, the juxtaposition of different types of behavior takes the pictorial image of hills and valleys, or ocean waves.

Hills and valleys and ocean waves represent the highs and lows of the human potential. The beauty of this second metaphor is in its ability to suggest that the way of life is to ride the waves, like an ocean surfer, all the way to the shore. Greater consciousness will facilitate this journey of life. The ability to ride the waves also reflects the potential duality of human nature.

Jewish Confessions

Many religious people, in lieu of riding the waves of life, feel constantly guilt-ridden. The guilt is associated with eating from some forbidden fruit and feeling expelled from the Garden of Eden. They fail to realize that it is the ongoing ebb and flow of life that is the norm.

Frequently, during pastoral rounds at Cedars-Sinai Medical Center, I listen to *confessions* from seriously ill Jewish patients. The Jewish confession usually deals with a "secret" that the patient has not revealed to anyone, not to a parent, not to clergy, not to a spouse and not to a friend. The word "secret" is in quotation marks because although the exact content of the secret has not been revealed, the underlying issue has become manifest through changed behavioral patterns. Interestingly, when the secret is ultimately shared and is heard in a non-judgmental manner, the patient sometimes feels comfortable in sharing the "secret" with significant others as well.

The patient feels guilt-ridden and views the illness as a punishment for acts of omission or commission that constitute the "secret." The guilt is ultimately based on an axiomatic, unitary view of human nature as necessarily good, obedient and altruistic. The opposite approach, which takes into account a dualistic view of human nature, transforms a guilt-ridden patient into one who rides the waves of life.

The same process applies to normally functioning, moderately depressed religious people who attend synagogue and conduct their lives in an observant Jewish fashion. In addition to guilt feelings that seem to be widespread in the Jewish community, many people seem to suffer from moderate to severe depression. This is not depression in the clinical psychological sense, but rather a lack of *joie de vivre*, life contentment and satisfaction.

The Jewish view, however, was expressed very beautifully by the Psalmist as "Serve God with happiness" (Psalms 100:2), including both inner contentment and outer happiness. Indeed, the theme of not serving God with happiness is suggested as one of the causes for myriad ills and curses that may befall the Jewish people (Deuteronomy 28:47): "Because you did not serve the Lord your God with joyfulness, and with gladness of heart..." However, it appears to me that this joyful attitude is rarely manifested. For many years now, I have observed both congregants and clergy during services in Reform, Conservative and Orthodox congregations. From these observations, I sometimes feel that the level of sadness and anger that appears in Jewish communal life, during services and related activities, is astonishing. The depression is ultimately based on an axiomatic, unitary view of life and human nature as necessarily being difficult, full of pain and suffering. As stated above, the opposite approach, which recognizes the dualistic view of human nature, can transform a depressed person into one who can ride the waves of life.

The ebb and flow of life refers to the alternating closeness to and distance from God that one experiences. During times of closeness, when one's feelings are similar to those of sincere friendship and being loved and beloved by God, human nature's manifestations are goodness par excellence. During times of distance, however, when one's feelings are akin to alienation, isolation and loneliness from God, human nature's manifestations are evil par excellence. This description of the ebb and flow of the alternating cycle of one's life is identical to the process of *Teshuvah* (repentance) as described by Maimonides (12th century) in his *Mishneh Torah* (*Hilkhot Teshuvah* 7:6). The process of repentance is highlighted for the masses of people between *Rosh Hashanah* and *Yom Kippur*, the ten-day period beginning with the Jewish New Year and concluding with the Day of Atonement. During this period, the apprehension of the Day of Atonement serves as an external motivating force to encourage people to repent. However, the essence of repentance takes place also throughout the year on a monthly, weekly and daily basis, and even within a given day. On a daily basis, there is always a fluctuation of thoughts, actions and intentions. Thus, the process of *Teshuvah* reflects the dual nature of each individual. *Teshuvah* is both a reflection of the *Yetzer ha-Ra* and *Yetzer ha-Tov*, and a concretization of the normalcy of the ebb and flow of life.

II.   Befriending Your Shadow

The dark and shadow side of individuals is usually completely denied, projected onto others or cognitively recognized and then suppressed. It is very unusual for it to be befriended. Yet, it is precisely through the process of befriending the shadow that ultimately, self-knowledge is attained. This self-knowledge creates greater self-consciousness, which leads to a greater realization of the Divine image within each individual. This greater consciousness transforms the dark side into an experience of potential new light and understanding.

Many individuals are completely unaware of possessing a dark and shadow side. They perceive themselves as primarily, and sometimes even exclusively, good-natured people. Frequently they project their shadow onto others, and they always find something negative in another person to criticize. As these good-natured people read this paragraph, they will not identify themselves as even being critical of others.   This lack of identification is a further indication of the denial of their shadow.   The Rabbis summarized this attitude in a pithy and succinct statement (Talmud, *Kiddushin* 70a):   *Kol ha-Poseil Pesul...be-Mumo Poseil* -- all who find deficiencies in others really see themselves in a mirror reflection.

Many other individuals are cognitively aware of their shadow, but either unintentionally repress or intentionally suppress it until they think it has disappeared.

All three categories of people -- those who deny the shadow categorically, those who project their shadow onto others and those who have repressed or suppressed their shadow -- lack the consciousness of the totality of life. Furthermore, and much more noticeably towards others, they act out the shadow in manipulative, narcissistic and hostile ways.

An alternative approach is what is referred to as befriending the shadow. Acknowledge it, embrace it, befriend it and dialogue with it. This shadow represents an integral part of each individual. The famous Socratic expression, "know thyself," also includes the negative, dark side of who one is. The dialogue with one's shadow can take the form of active imagination, whereby an imaginary dialogue takes place between two people, each of whom is an integral part of the same person. This dialogue is not an easy conversation, but it is necessary and it heightens one's understanding of oneself.

Another advantage of discovering this shadow is that the issues are amplified, and the shadow and the dialogue become part of a larger whole than the immediacy of guilt, shame and other feelings that accompany the particular issue at hand. Once an issue is amplified, a relaxed feeling hovers over the individual, the stress level is diminished and the difficult decision that lies in front of the individual evaporates into the air, as new possibilities emerge. During this dialogue, the psyche reaches new heights of consciousness, and a certain inner transformation is achieved. The discomfort of the shadow is transformed into an inner air of tranquility, serenity and vision. This inner vision creates a new psychic reality, as opposed to a physical reality. This psychic reality has no dimensions, and it is potentially limitless and without boundaries. Ultimately it reflects an aspect of the soul and a new depth of existence. I am privileged to share part of a journal entry by one of my clients. It is entitled *Shadow Talk: A Dialogue with Myself*.

*****

Shadow Talk: A Dialogue with Myself

Hearing a noise at my door, I glanced up quickly only to see no one standing there. I was quite sure someone was in the next room as I could sense the presence of another, but whoever was there was not anxious to show herself. I got up from my desk, walked to the door, and looked into my living room. You might have expected me to be surprised or frightened by the figure I saw lounging on my couch uninvited, and so I was. However, this being my house and my world, I felt compelled to stand firm and demand an explanation for her presence.

"Who are you and what are you doing in my house?"

"My, my, we are a nervous little creature, aren't we," she said in a tone as condescending as it was sultry, "Don't worry, I won't hurt you."

I wasn't sure I believed her. There was an air of danger about this woman, a presence that surrounded her like the energy of a cat about to spring, taut, tense, controlled and yet untamed. She sat back on my couch, clearly enjoying my discomfort, and stroked the silky, black satin of her sexy dress with studied abandon.

"Why don't you sit down and relax?"

"How did you get in here?," I said, glancing at the door which was clearly still locked from the inside.

"Hmmm...not only are we nervous, but we ask stupid questions, too."

"Considering you're trespassing in my domain, you might at least do me the courtesy of answering my questions."

"Trespassing?," she laughed in a voice that dripped with honey and poison. "Why, I live here, too, sweetheart, or hadn't you noticed?"

"You don't live here. You're lying."

"I may be presumptuous but I'm not a liar. My truths may be as black as night but they are not lies."

"All right, if you live here, how come I haven't ever seen you here before?"

"Oh, you have, but you are the one who lies. Isn't pretending you don't see someone a lie?"

"How could I pretend not to see you when I don't even know who you are?"

"Oh, don't play dumb with me, Antonia. You know perfectly well who I am. Why don't you just admit it, and save us both the bother of continuing this dull interchange."

I headed for the door and put my hand on the knob.

"Leave now, and we'll just pretend this little meeting never took place. I'll forget about you and you forget about me and we'll both live happily ever after."

She just smiled as the knob turned impotently in my hand and wouldn't unlock the door. Try as I might, I could not open the door. There was no way out.

I turned to her and yelled furiously, "What kind of a game are you playing? It's not even original. Sartre thought of it first in *No Exit*. Why don't you give it up; it's stupid."

"Well, you may be dull, Antonia, but at least you're not illiterate. Why don't you sit down?"

"Thank you very much," I said acidly, and stomped over to a chair into which I sank, resigned to the fact that I was indeed trapped in this room with this woman. All right, I thought defiantly, I may be stuck here but I still don't have to talk to her.

"But, I can hear your every thought, and you can hear mine, so you cannot help but talk to me, even though you don't want to. Now that you know I'm here you must communicate with me, you have no choice."

"There is always a choice," I muttered, "and besides I haven't even acknowledged knowing you yet."

"You know who I am. Just take a closer look, Antonia. You're not blind, yet, in fact your vision is better than most if you'd take off your self-imposed blinders."

I didn't want to look at her. The thought of meeting this stranger's eyes was so painful I could not face it right away. So I stared at her feet for a while. She had slim ankles and thin but shapely legs. Kind of sexy, I thought, immediately chastising myself for the thought.

"So you like my legs, that's nice, what else do you like, Antonia?," she crooned lasciviously.

"Nothing." I crossed my arms tightly in front of me and stared at the floor again.

"Come on, give in to the urge. Why don't you look at all of me? I'm waiting just for you."

"I don't want to."

"Yes, you do. You're just being stubborn and perverse."

"I'm perverse?" If I'm perverse then what are you?," I spat at her.

"I'm what's real. I am your flesh, the corporeal side of your nature. I am desire and lust. I am wanton and wanting. I am greed, and hunger, impatience and ambition. I am jealousy and need. I am the side of you that covets other women's husbands -- even your own mother's. I am pleasure and heat, sex and sin, adultery and incest, touch and sensation. I am all you fancy but don't have the guts or will to go after. I am..."

"You may think you are all those things, in fact you may be all of them, too, but that doesn't mean I want all those things."

"You still can't admit it to yourself, can you? And you think I have an ego problem."

"Why do I need to admit it to myself if you know it all already?"

"Don't you know?"

"No."

"Well, Antonia dear, I see we have a lot of talking to do."

"Why don't you just tell me and put me out of my misery?"

"That wouldn't be half as much fun," she said with her cruel smile, watching me squirm under her gaze.

"I don't want to talk to you," I said sullenly.

"I can see that you don't. In fact, I can also see that you have the urge to kill me. Why don't you try? I dare you."

Startled with the truth of her statement, I almost threw myself at her but caught myself just in time.

"Sorry, I'm not that stupid. Killing you is the same as giving in to you and I won't give you the satisfaction."

She laughed again. "I see you are a formidable opponent. But so am I, and we have just begun to wrestle, you and I. Who knows who will prevail at dawn, if there is a dawn beyond this locked and lonely room. I have the power of darkness and shadow on my side, so beware."

Despite my attempt to keep a brave and impassive front, I could feel fear and its strangling cold make its paralyzing way up my body. I shivered, unable to hide the terror I felt inside, while she sat there looking smug and self-satisfied, as if the battle was as good as won. I wasn't entirely sure it hadn't been.

*****

When this shadow dialogue is continued, new conflicts may emerge; however, as a result of this process, a new inner peace can ultimately be achieved. One sees the shadow as part of a larger cosmos, a perception that leads to a feeling of unity with all of humanity.

Befriending our Image of "God's Shadow"

The same active imagination that is used in creating greater consciousness regarding an individual's shadow can be utilized in befriending God's shadow as well. Dialoguing with God's shadow can also create greater consciousness, although this sometimes emerges at great personal sacrifice. Jacob, our Patriarch, struggled with a Divine encounter. He limped for the rest of his life, but as a result of the encounter, he saw God face to face and his soul was saved (Genesis 32:31). This discussion of "God's shadow" utilizes a metaphor based on the human psyche (Jung, *CW*, v. 11). This is not meant as a theological or metaphysical analysis of this issue.

Most people are afraid to dialogue with God, although they pray to God on a regular basis. Among the various patients who have consulted me as Chaplain at Cedars-Sinai Medical Center, a 72-year-old, Polish-born American Jewish woman typifies the inability of many to dialogue with God. This emaciated, bright lady, diagnosed with a severe case of bronchial pneumonia, asked me to pray with her for a complete and speedy recovery. At the conclusion of the pastoral visit, she asked me why she was suffering so much. After asking her what she felt and thought about her question, I asked her to include this question in her evening prayers, to see how God would respond. With complete sincerity, she replied, "Do you mean that God will answer me?" I stretched out my hand to hold her hand and I said, "I hope that God will answer you tonight." She continued and asked, "Will I actually *hear* God's answer? Isn't prayer a monologue?" I replied, "You will hear God's response, but it will be with your inner ear, and it will listen to your inner voice, which represents your Divine image of God." She nodded her head as if she understood what I meant, and I left.

Here was a religious woman who had prayed on a regular basis for some 70 years and never really dialogued with God. For her, God was not a *living* reality.

Just as Jacob dialogued with God, many people can imaginatively and creatively dialogue with God. Individuals can achieve greater consciousness as the Divine image is encountered. This may be a difficult process, but in this way it is possible to befriend God's shadow.

III. Heroic Behavior

Many people act heroically. Their heroism takes many different forms. For some it is a creative dialogue with the shadow and light sides of God, and for some it is a significant change in life as a response to a crisis in life.

One patient, whom I was privileged to serve as Rabbi, creatively dialogued with God regarding his cancer. He claimed that he and God together would not be the victims of cancer, but rather, they would courageously and valiantly fight the disease together. Although he eventually succumbed to the illness, he maintained the vigor of his mind until the end. He was not fighting with God; he was allied with God in fighting the cancer. (For an elaboration of this person's inspiring inner resources, see Erwin Altman's "Reflections on this Thing and *No-Thing* Called Life and Death" in Meier, 1988.)

The following patients were all facing life-threatening illnesses and were able to manifest their heroic attitudes in the following ways (Blau, 1989):

• David Coons was diagnosed with lymphoma. His heroic attitude was expressed by, "Just be real optimistic."

• Cecilia Succetti was diagnosed with breast cancer, which had spread to her lymph nodes. Her heroic attitude was expressed by, "I appreciate things more now and try to tell people I love them more often instead of just thinking that they're going to know that. I don't take things for granted so much."

• James Stone was diagnosed with cancer, and his heroic attitude was expressed by, "If I could change my life, I would have done more to create better understanding around the conflict that is going on between the races and why people are poor."

• Irving Kaplan was diagnosed with prostate cancer, and his heroic attitude was expressed by, "To live means to appreciate the precious stimulation, meaning an involvement or awareness."

• Linda Zarins was diagnosed with ALS (Lou Gehrig's disease), and her heroic attitude was expressed by, "If I'm lucky, I'll choke on a croissant. If I'm not lucky, I'll be in the hospice on a lot of Valium and just go under."

- Ann Miller was diagnosed with leukemia, and her heroic attitude was expressed by, "I just try to live the best I can every day -- to make the best out of every day and not worry about what's going to happen tomorrow." Her husband, Earl Miller, responded to her illness by stating that her illness "brought us closer together."

- Candelaria Cruz was diagnosed with cancer, and her heroic attitude was expressed by, "I'm just paying attention to whatever I'm doing."

- Clifford Daniel was diagnosed with cancer, and his heroic attitude was expressed by, "I don't think any two people are alike when it comes to life. I can't tell anybody anything about how to live or how to go through this illness."

- Robert Cyr was diagnosed with AIDS, and his heroic attitude was expressed by, "The reaction from my friends has been so positive that it has changed my life. I've become more alive in the last three weeks. I know that death is a part of a continuation, it's not an end. I've discovered in the height of my illness that I can sit down and write plays and comedies. I want to do something that's rather uplifting and inspirational."

- Carol Redding was diagnosed with leukemia, and her heroic attitude was expressed by, "I began to reassess what I felt was important in my life. I promised myself that I would not talk to any relatives I really didn't like. I promised myself that if I ever got well enough, I would leave my job and find a job that was more fulfilling."

- Nancy Sawhney was diagnosed with cancer, and her heroic attitude was expressed by, "It's a real adventure to have a physical disability and a progressive disease. It's simply as if you are driving down the road of life and all of a sudden you've gone off on a route that you never anticipated. You take it and it's truly an adventure."

- Rhonda Gelbman was diagnosed with a tumor in the sinus cavity, and her heroic attitude was expressed by, "If I only have two months, a year, or whatever it is, I want to make the best of it."

- Vera Humburg was diagnosed with colon cancer, and her heroic attitude was expressed by, "So, I stop and smell the roses a lot more now. I just live each day a little more fully."

- Edward Hopster was diagnosed with cancer, and his heroic attitude was expressed by, "Just live from day to day, that's all. Enjoy the years you got left."

- Fred Clark was diagnosed with ALS, and his heroic attitude was expressed by, "I seem to have closer friends now than I had before, but my closest friends are people I wasn't close to before."

- Mildred Gavlin was diagnosed with a life-threatening illness, and her heroic attitude was expressed by, "I think the answer is to take each day as it comes."

- Joe Kogel was diagnosed with malignant melanoma, and his heroic attitude was expressed by, "I learned there is a way of being alive that is so much richer and brighter than anything I'd imagined. The issue now is, how do I live there without cancer" (L.A. Times, September 6, 1989, Part V, pp. 1-2).

- Dennis Reddish was diagnosed with cancer, and his heroic attitude was expressed by, "This disease has changed my life, and I have changed my life. I went out and bought a sailboat, which I've been putting off for five years."

- Virginia Gomez was diagnosed with cancer, and her heroic attitude was expressed by, "This is the time to slow down and enjoy life. My relationship with my husband has improved, we have gotten closer. My children also seem to express their feelings a little bit more. Now they tell me their feelings and beautiful thoughts. They also tell me how much they admire me and really appreciate what I have taught them."

- Sherri Marsh was diagnosed with stomach cancer, and her heroic attitude was expressed by, "I realize that the relationships between people are a lot more important, and we certainly have grown a lot closer together. Another thing that helps me tremendously is that some of the funniest things in my life have happened when people found out I've had cancer."

All these people and many more are real heroes of life. I hope and pray that these heroes will be granted sufficient time to implement their new heroic attitudes towards life. Having said that, I feel sad that the examples selected were all patients who were facing a life-threatening illness and only as a result of that awareness became acutely cognizant of the finiteness of life and their own mortality.

Zest for Life

I would like to suggest an alternative hero archetype that would be applicable to all people, those who are patients and those who are not yet patients, those whom our society sometimes refers to as "healthy." Both categories of people can be acutely aware of their own mortality and of the finiteness of life.

The new category of heroes is for those who have a *zest for life*. Zest for life refers to experiencing each moment to its fullest, and not reflecting on yesterday or anticipating tomorrow, but rather living in the here-and-now. This heroic attitude requires attentive consciousness, awareness, openness to that which is unexpected and the ability to focus and concentrate.

The zest for life begins when one first awakes in the morning and says "Good morning" to members of the family. Is it said with a smile, and what is the volume, pitch and tone utilized to articulate this communication? Is there eye contact during this communication? What is the feeling in the heart and soul when these words are expressed? Is it synonymous with, antithetical to or neutral in regard to the meaning of the expression? Is it followed or preceded by an embrace or kiss?

This "Good morning" also creates a brief I-Thou relationship between the two people (Buber, 1958). Both people, the person who initiates the "Good morning" and the person who responds, become conscious of self, the other, the relationship and the emotional feelings present between them. Do the emotional feelings encompass love and friendship, or do they create a sense of isolation and alienation?

This I-Thou relationship and the "Good morning" expression are also affected by whether this person woke up late, early or at the usual time to get to work on time. Or, is this morning a *Shabbat* (Sabbath) or a special Jewish holiday, when a different emotion is applicable? Furthermore, have either of these two people dreamt during the night, and do they keep a journal of their dreams? And how does each person feel physically, emotionally, spiritually and psychologically? Is the "Good morning" verbalized, but in a habitual manner?

Furthermore, the expression "Good morning" also represents the duality of each individual. The word "good" only has meaning when its linguistic opposite comes to mind. The word "morning" also brings to mind night, when darkness and shadow emerge.

This analysis of one moment in one day exemplifies the *zest for life* approach. Just as the patients who are facing life-threatening illnesses were able to express their heroic attitudes under the most difficult of circumstances, so also this second category of *zest for life* heroes comprises ordinary people who have the potential to rise to the occasion and live each moment in the most authentic, full and complete way. This attitude frequently emerges when a person is able to face the unconscious. Such an attitude is also heroic because it requires the awareness and realization that these healthy people are mortal and that this life is finite.

This *zest for life* attitude requires the ability to *experience* the moment and not just go through the motions, which at times may become habitual. The prophet Isaiah (29:13) lamented that not only "Good morning" greetings become habitual, but even the performance of Divine commandments frequently becomes automatic, without an essential understanding of the *Mitzvah* (commandment) or the experience of the moment. Isaiah referred to this deficiency and inadequacy as *Mitzvat Anashim Melumada*, that is, the practice of *Mitzvot* (commandments) which remain in the realm of an intellectual, habitual exercise.

An example of the aforementioned practice is whether and how a guest is welcomed in a synagogue. One of my colleagues from the East Coast was visiting in Los Angeles for a week. As was his regular custom, he attended one of the neighborhood synagogues on a daily basis to pray with a *Minyan* (quorum). Subsequently, he shared with me his experience that not one of his fellow parishioners had come over to him to welcome him with a greeting of "*Shalom Aleikhem*" (peace be unto you).

How contrary this behavior is to the spirit of Judaism may be derived from the episode when God appeared unto Abraham, and Abraham interrupted God's dialogue with him to welcome three strangers (Genesis 18:1-2). What has happened to contemporary Jewish practices? The spirit is often lost. The Jew is not even in search of a soul anymore. He has been transformed into an automaton who recites meaningless phrases such as, "Happy are those who dwell in Your House" (Psalms 84:5), without being cognizant of who is dwelling or sitting or visiting this House of God.

Isaiah's lamentation can, in essence, be proclaimed again, "Why are you so meticulous in the rituals and sacrifices you offer to God, if your hands are full of blood, the heart is frozen and the spirit is lost?" (Isaiah 1:11-15).

In contrast, the *zest for life* approach can be continued throughout one's day, week, month, year and life, with endless examples of expected and unexpected events in one's life. This *zest for life* heroic approach requires the ongoing development and growth of each individual in all dimensions. Biological, psychological, spiritual and emotional growth are all necessary components in the lifelong process of living. This *zest for life* approach is also a *natural* way for life to evolve.

The following will serve as additional examples of a heroic attitude towards life by those who live with zest. In contrast to the real-life examples of common heroes who face life-threatening illnesses, the following examples represent composites of hundreds of patients and clients who have crossed my path during the last twenty years.

_____ was diagnosed as having a depressive neurosis, which she associated with her parents who were emotionally abusive. Her heroic attitude was expressed by her disentangling herself from her abusive parents and individuating on her own path.

_____ was diagnosed as unable to develop and form intimate heterosexual relationships due to sexual abuse by her uncle when she was a child. Her heroic attitude was expressed by completely "Going forth" (Genesis 12:1) from the mores, customs and culture of her home of origin and establishing her own home. Ultimately, she formed an intimate relationship with another person.

_____ was the sister of a paranoid schizophrenic. Her heroic attitude was expressed by her being able to differentiate between caring for a sister and being similar to a sister. Her path became clear as she became an attorney.

_____ was diagnosed as having hypertension associated with diabetes. His heroic attitude was expressed by his learning to cope with a chronic illness and live a near-normal life.

_____ was diagnosed as always being in a rush, associated with a high degree of anxiety. His heroic attitude was expressed by his slowing down his pace so he could "smell the roses."

_____ was diagnosed as having a low self-worth and a low self-esteem, despite her many prestigious professional accomplishments and a personally-fulfilled life. Her heroic attitude was expressed by her letting go of her ego and not living her life in anticipation of the accolades of others. Her unconscious was awakened, her external accomplishments declined and her happiness increased.

_____ was diagnosed as having a poor self-image, associated with obesity. Despite frequent weight losses, she always returned to her previous weight. The secondary gain from her obese condition was the attention that others paid her. At the same time, the obesity gave her "valid excuses" for not developing an intimate relationship with others. Her heroic response was to develop zest for life, here-and-now. She said, "I now realize that life is not a rehearsal; it is now!" She allowed her vulnerabilities to be expressed and realized that her vulnerabilities allowed for appropriate intimacy. Ultimately she lost weight, and her self-image improved significantly.

_____ was diagnosed as an Amazon woman. She alienated her family and friends and bitterly complained how unappreciative everyone was of her generosity. She was completely unconscious of her manipulative and narcissistic personality. Her heroic attitude was finally expressed in her seventh decade of life when she took a bold step and entered therapy. As her therapy proceeded, *her needs* became more apparent to her family and friends, and her isolation was transformed into new and meaningful friendships.

_____ was diagnosed as having an obsessive-compulsive personality. He was a very successful attorney residing in Beverly Hills. He explained that he needed to compulsively put everything in order in his very chaotic world. His heroic attitude was expressed by his gradually accepting the chaos in the world. Initially, this path was extremely difficult for him, but ultimately it allowed him a much more spontaneous and happy lifestyle.

All these people responded to treatment and developed a zest for life by overcoming tremendous impediments and obstacles. These people were truly heroes, and they were not shameful about realistically seeing their situations cognitively and emotionally, and then changing their inner visions and subsequently, their external behaviors.

IV. Shamefulness, Embarrassment and Stagnation

There are two colloquial expressions that depict the reason why many people are unable to live life with zest. The first general expression is, "I want to eat my cake and have it too," and the second is, "*Doctor*, please do anything, but take the pain away." The implication is that the individual wants *everything* but does not want to sacrifice or change anything about his or her lifestyle. After close to twenty years of pastoral and psychological counseling, I have found that one main theme emerges. Most patients and clients express their concerns and worries as follows:

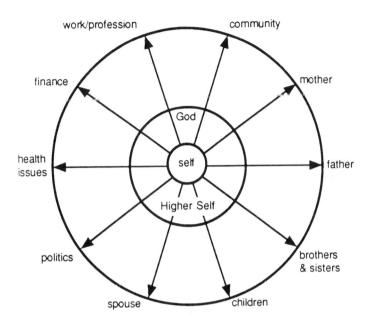

The individual is at the center of a wheel having approximately ten spokes, each one representing an external issue that needs to be changed in order for the individual to feel better. Surrounding the self is the constant, yet dynamic image of a Higher Self, based on one's image of God. The individual does not want to change, but naively wants the assistance of the psychologist to change the externals, the ten spokes. It may very well be that the externals are real issues, and some of the difficult relationships may be due to pathologies of others, but nevertheless, the changes that need to take place must come from the center of the wheel, the individual. However, most clients resist any change, either in external behavior or in the psyche and in their perceptions of reality. There is immense stagnation and resistance. Clients feel too embarrassed to modify their behavior and too shameful to acknowledge their responsibility for all of their choices in life. Many want to keep their exact roles within their families and in relation to their friends. They desperately want to eliminate the psychic pain, but they are unable to make the necessary changes.

The shamefulness rests in the awareness that God has given the gift of life, and this life has become sterile. The transformation of self to Higher Self will facilitate a constantly new perspective vis-a-vis the issues of life.

Although biological death is what many people fear and are confused about, there is another death, which perhaps is more significant. That is what dies within the potential of each individual during one's lifetime and is never realized.

The Supreme Heroic Attitude

The supreme heroic attitude is the continued growth and development of the self throughout life. This heroic attitude is characterized by each individual's process of individuation, which is lifelong. Complacency with mere survival represents a cowardly attitude. Each individual has the key to release the prisoner of childhood, with which so many clients identify. Individuals can ultimately honor their fathers and mothers specifically by becoming fully mature adults. When this process takes place, the Self at the center of the circle feels satisfied, and the issues on the circumference of the circle fade in significance as the unconscious continues to awaken more and more. The continuous development of the unconscious allows one to experience the multifaceted aspects of ordinary life on a deeper and deeper level.

The creation story indicates that darkness preceded the creation of light. However, there was one other aspect that coexisted with the infinite God and the spirit of God, and that is water (Genesis 1:2).

The spirit of God hovered over water. The symbol of water often represents the deepening and the depth of the unconscious. Indeed, the Talmud, which reflects aspects of the unconscious, is also referred to as "The Ocean of the Talmud." The spirit of God not only hovers over the water, but also hovers over the symbolic natural element of creativity, the unconscious.

The birthing process of each individual begins with the breaking of the water of the amniotic sac. This birthing process is lifelong, as more and more water is divided as one continues to explore the unconscious.

The birthing process that takes place continuously on an individual level also takes place intermittently on a collective level. The physical exodus of the Jewish people from Egypt was inadequate to prepare them for the Divine Revelation at Mount Sinai. They needed a deepening of their individual and collective consciousness. The same element of water that preceded the creation of the world was present as the Jewish people journeyed to Sinai. They entered the depth of the Sea of Reeds, and water surrounded them from all sides. This experience immediately awakened the people to sing and dance, new outward manifestations of their awakening souls.

Darkness gives way to light, and water is the medium for the investigation of the depth of life through the deepening of consciousness. The individual who pursues this path is the hero, while the individual who never learns how to swim physically survives and exists, but does not fully appreciate God's supreme gift -- the spirit of God that continuously hovers above and in the depth of water.

I started this chapter with an analogy of the sun rising in the east and setting in the west. This image is contrasted to one's shadow rising in the west and setting in the east. Only at noontime, when the sun is most bright, is the shadow eclipsed completely. Then, when the shadow is not visible, is specifically when darkness needs to be recognized and identified. The reverse is also true. When one goes to sleep, the atmosphere is tranquil and serene. There is physical tiredness and complete darkness. It is precisely at that time that dreams become the beacon of light. It is precisely out of the darkness of nighttime sleep that the inner pictorial dream images shed light on one's entire life. It is precisely then, at the moments and hours of darkness, that the spirit of God, in the form of dreams, hovers over each individual to help everyone individuate and strive for *zest for life*!

V.   Darkness, Ruach (God's Spirit) and Water

Before the beginning of creation, darkness and water coexisted with God's spirit (Genesis 1:2). The first action that is recorded in the Bible is God's being creative (*Bara*, Genesis 1:1), and we are asked to emulate those actions of creativity (Deuteronomy 28:9). From the state of darkness, God created light. From the element of water, God created the upper waters, the heavens and the lower waters, the oceans. From God's Spirit, the process of God's expansion begins and culminates with God's Spirit taking the form of the image of God implanted in humanity.

Similarly, as we emulate God's behavior, we create light from darkness, we create a deepening of consciousness from the waters of the unconscious, and the soul's never-ending expansion correlates with the expansion of God's spirit.

The process of individuation, which means the lifelong process of becoming and fulfilling our unique potential, depends on our ability to utilize these three elements -- darkness, spirit and water -- which have existed from before time, in order to help each individual create his or her own destiny.

There is no end to the darkness that each individual encounters in life -- from mental anguish to physical pain, from feelings of lack of self-worth to acts of violence, from perceived failures to feelings of being rejected and abandoned, from feelings of isolation and alienation from God and people to countless more accounts of the vast unhappiness of so many people. Yet it is precisely from this darkness that a new light can come to help everyone with this process of individuation. Mental anguish and physical pain create greater sensitivity to others who are suffering and give one the ability to appreciate a life of serenity and health.

Feelings of lack of self-worth, which are universal, can be ascribed to an inferior function, i.e., to the parts of one's self that really are inferior. The recognition of the existence of an inferior function can eventually lead to self-acceptance. The realm of the inferior functions is where people are emotional, touchy and unadapted, and they therefore acquire the habit of covering up this part of their personality (Von Franz, 1971). As individuals gain greater understanding of their unconscious, their feelings of lack of self-worth can be ascribed to an inferior function, which makes the bridge to the unconscious. Similarly, if acts of violence have been perpetrated against any individual, this person can be more able to identify with the potential violence that is generic to everyone. Also, feelings of rejection can eventually lead to being more tolerant and accepting of all people with deficiencies and inadequacies. Feelings of isolation and alienation can lead to feelings of closeness to God. The Talmud (*Berakhot* 34b) states: "People who have repented are on a higher level (of holiness) than people who have always been righteous." From the darkness comes light, but only if the person individuates and sees life and all of the circumstances as unique and distinctive. No prescribed role is dictated; no master plan is revealed other than the specific path that emerges. No son is identical to his father and no daughter is exactly like her mother. No younger sister is identical to her older sister or brother. No younger brother is identical to his older brother or sister. Each person creates his or her own world, and this world unfolds as life proceeds.

The Spirit of God is implanted in each person as the image of God. This Spirit represents the divine spark in everyone. It allows the individual to experience the divine in the ordinary. Eyes and ears are capable of seeing and hearing. However, the eyes can also see in a divine way, and the ears can hear in a divine way. This special way requires that each person individuate to achieve his or her own unique images of God.

The darkness can be transformed into light, and the spirit of God can open up new dimensions of life when each individual is willing to swim in the waters of the unconscious. Sometimes the waters may be rough and sometimes calm. When one rides the waves, the ebb and flow, the ups and downs and the highs and lows, then one lives life guided by God. The birthing process never stops. Even death is experienced as a transition to a new birth of complete spirituality with the Spirit of God.

References

Blau, E. (1989). *Common heroes: Facing a life threatening illness.* Pasadena: NewSage Press.

Buber, M. (1958). *I and thou.* 2nd ed. Translated by Ronald Gregor Smith. New York: Charles Scribner's Sons.

Hirsch, S.R. (1976). *The Pentateuch.* Gateshead, England: Judaica Press.

The Holy Scriptures. (3 vols.) (1982). Philadelphia: Jewish Publication Society.

Jung, C.G. (20 vols.) (1969). *Collected works.* Princeton, N.J.: Princeton University Press.

Maimonides, M. (12th century) (1962). *Mishneh Torah* (6 vols.). New York: M.P. Press.

Meier, L. (1988). *Jewish values in psychotherapy: Essays on vital issues on the search for meaning.* Lanham, MD: University Press of America.

The Talmud (18 vols.) (1961). I. Epstein (Ed.). London: Soncino Press.

Von Franz, M.L. and Hillman, J. (1971). *Jung's typology.* Zurich: Spring Publications.

CHAPTER VI

A PSYCHOLOGICAL MIDRASH

GOD'S STRUGGLE WITH MAN: JACOB AND THE LONELY NIGHT JOURNEY

Genesis 32:25-33: "And Jacob was left alone, and an *Ish* struggled with him until dawn. And the *Ish* saw that he could not overcome Jacob, and he touched the cavity of Jacob's thigh, and he dislodged Jacob's hip joint as he was struggling with him. And the *Ish* said: 'Let me go, for dawn has already arrived,' and Jacob said to the *Ish*: 'Our struggle will continue into daylight until you bless me.' And the *Ish* said to Jacob: 'What is your name?,' and he said: 'My name is Jacob.' And the *Ish* said: 'Jacob shall not be your exclusive name; you will also be known as Israel, because you have prevailed with God and with men.' And Jacob asked the *Ish*: 'Please tell me your name,' and the *Ish* said: 'Why are you asking for my name?,' and the *Ish* blessed Jacob there. And Jacob designated the name of the place as Peniel, which acknowledged that 'I was privileged to see God face to face, and my life was spared.' And as Jacob passed Penuel, the sun shone for him, and Jacob limped on his thigh. Therefore, the Children of Israel shall forever not eat the sinew of the thigh-vein, which is on the hollow of the thigh, precisely because the *Ish* dislodged the hollow of Jacob's thigh, in the thigh-vein."

I

Introduction

I have always been perplexed by the fact that the Jewish people are known as *Bnei Yisrael* (the Children of Israel). It is self-evident that the term "Children of Israel" derives from the fact that the children of Jacob (Israel) became the Twelve Tribes of Israel. My query, however, is an attempt to understand this appellation on a more profound level.   For example, one could hypothesize that the name for the Jewish people might be *Bnei Avraham* (the Children of Abraham) or *Bnei Moshe* (the Children of Moses).

After all, Abraham was the first person to rediscover monotheism and was also known as the Father of nations.   One of his attributes was that he performed acts of lovingkindness.   So the name "Children of Abraham" would have served as an inspiration to future generations.   Furthermore, Abraham also went through a metamorphosis.   First, he was known as Avram.   Then his name was changed to reflect his mission to the world and his essence, i.e., the Father of all nations (Genesis 17:5).

Similarly, the name "Children of Moses" also seems appropriate. Moses was the greatest of all the Prophets, and he served as the mediator between God and the Jewish people at the time of Revelation and the giving of the Torah.

But the Jewish people are not known by the names of these ancestors, although interestingly, our Christian and Islamic brethren frequently refer to the Jewish people as the Children of Abraham.   We refer to ourselves exclusively as the *Bnei Yisrael* (Children of Israel).   Despite this appellation, when the blessings are given to the Twelve Tribes by their father (Genesis 49), he is referred to as Jacob, not Israel.   Perhaps this choice of names is to illustrate that in achieving the fulfillment of these blessings, each of us needs to work through our own process of becoming who we are destined to be.

One of the first times that we are referred to as the Children of Israel is in Genesis (46:8), when the Bible enumerates those who go down to Egypt.   Apparently, this reference suggests the importance of the descent into Egypt, as well as the essence of what Israel actually stands for.   That essence will serve as the vehicle for the future redemption from exile.

The descent into Egypt may be understood on many levels.   First, though the Children of Israel were uprooted from their own land, Egypt initially provided them with material sustenance.   Second, the etymology of the Hebrew word for Egypt (*Mitzrayim*) is related to the word *tzar* ("narrow," "dangerous"), perhaps signifying that the people were entering narrow and dangerous straits, a place of oppression and difficulties. Third, the name of Egypt is associated with what happened there, i.e., an enslavement that was both physical and psychological.

In order to understand what the "Children of Israel" signifies regarding the individual and collective destiny of the people, we need to understand the change of name from "Jacob our Patriarch" to Israel. We must also keep in mind that one name was not totally eclipsed in favor of the other. Israel was bestowed as an additional name for Jacob. Thus, when we refer to Jacob, we are aware that we also refer to Israel, and vice versa.

How did Jacob come to also be Israel? While Jacob was preparing to meet his brother, he experienced a *numinous* event that ultimately would change the entire direction of his own path, as well as that of the entire Jewish people.

Prior to Jacob's encounter during the night, he found himself entirely alone. The thoughts that passed through his mind at that silent and lonely time might have included a review of his entire life until then. This was a mid-life evaluation of who he was, a survey of his goals and reflections about his lineage, i.e., his parents and grandparents.

His questions to himself might have included the following: "What was my destiny supposed to be as the twin born second, holding on to the heel of Esau? Was sibling rivalry a motivating factor in my obtaining the birthright? Was I preying on the vulnerability of my brother, who was tired and hungry? Why did I listen to my mother and receive the blessing of my father, when Esau was out doing my father's bidding? More perplexing, who was my father and who was my mother? Was my father, Isaac, really spared, or was a part of him symbolically sacrificed on the altar? Was he a victor or a victim? Why didn't my father and mother communicate about such crucial matters?" Interestingly, only one conversation between Isaac and Rebeccah is recorded in the Bible, in Genesis 27:46.

"I understand that my mother received a prophecy regarding the blessing that was to be bestowed upon me. Is prophecy supposed to be kept a secret between husband and wife? Does the course of destiny trample on marital etiquette in a relationship? Can a blessing emerge out of secrecy?

Perhaps when I meet my brother, Esau, he actually will kill me, and I will die prematurely. Has my life been fulfilled? Have I been honest with myself, with my family, with God? I recognize that God has given me unparalleled visionary opportunities -- a Ladder of Ascension; Isaac for a father; Abraham for a grandfather; a lineage that is blessed."

Jacob's encounter with Esau after he crosses the Yabok River finds its symbolism represented in each of our lives as well. We are engaged in a continual process of self-evaluation. We ask ourselves similar questions before the major encounters in our lives.

These encounters do not have to involve confrontations with brothers or other family members bent on murder. They can involve, for example, issues such as illness, bankruptcy, aloneness, loneliness, depression, anxiety or mere fright.

At its core, the encounter between Jacob and Esau focuses on the fear of the other.   Jacob perceives Esau as someone who is bigger, more powerful and more authoritative than he. Moreover, he recognizes that Esau is someone with whom he consciously or unconsciously acted in bad faith, and someone whom he hugged and kissed, but perhaps not wholeheartedly.

"People know me as a person who dwells in tents, studying and meditating. But there is another side of me as well. I am jealous of my brother; I do not know how to hunt, as he does. Furthermore, why did my father love my brother, while my mother loved me? There is a dark side of me that is not revealed to others, but is known to me. I wanted to marry Rachel; she is my beloved. But first I had to marry Leah. My uncle tricked me. Just look at my uncle's name, Laban. It means "white," signifying purity. To outsiders, he is known as 'pure,' but he cheated me. Perhaps I focused on my uncle's externals, with too much trust.

"Then what did God do? My favorite wife was barren, and I kept having children that I initially did not want. I am confused. I love and I do not love. My destiny often seems to be at odds with my desires. What good was my dream about the Ladder of Ascension if it was followed by Laban ('White') being deceitful to me?

"Here I am, stuck at the Yabok river, with many confusing and bothersome thoughts. Maybe I should end my life. Or, perhaps the water is here to remind me of its symbolism for life, creation and the unconscious. Furthermore, I know that I am not supposed to die here. By its name, the Yabok (from the root, *avak*, 'to struggle') tells me that I am here merely to struggle.

"Perhaps what will happen between me and my brother will foretell the history of the world. Why must the blessing that my father gave be through 'me' alone and not through 'us?' Maybe I can create an 'us.' My struggles and thoughts will play a role in the destiny of the Jewish people and the world. But perhaps I am not in charge, as I have seen, for instance, regarding my marriage. Perhaps Divine Providence will guide me on my way. Before the Dream of Ascension, I prayed to God, and now, before my encounter in the night, I am all alone again, to pray to God."

Reflections on the Struggle

One of the reasons that this section of the Torah is significant for me, particularly in my adulthood, is related to the date on which this portion is read annually in the synagogue. Eighteen days after my father went into a coma, following a heart attack, he died on the 17th of the Hebrew month of Kislev. The anniversary of his death (*Yahrzeit*) usually falls on or near the Sabbath on which the portion that includes these verses is read. For each of these eighteen years since his death, I have been asked to give a Torah-related talk or lesson related to this section. It is as if God has asked me to look at these passages with particular care.

Does individual growth take place with family members present, or with rabbis or doctors present, or does it take place when one is alone? Before the world was created, how did God feel? Was He lonely or alone? Was His feeling of loneliness alleviated through creating other entities, or was the loneliness accentuated by the qualitative differences between God and His creations? Does God continue to be alone? Is God in search of man, or vice versa? Or both?

Jacob was alone, both physically and spiritually. Sometimes, one can be alone and not lonely. One can also be lonely, even though not alone. Jacob felt both lonely and alone.

Are loneliness and aloneness a deviation, or are they the norm of an ordinary life? Although we, as a society, place emphasis and value on friendship, family, local community and world community, ultimately we live in solitude, constantly reflecting, contemplating, even while enjoying life.

To some, the word "solitude" has negative connotations, but this term is not used here in a negative sense. Rather, it is meant to convey an empirical, psychological observation about life. It is meant to illustrate the specialness, uniqueness and distinctiveness of each individual's psyche and private thoughts.

Even in intimacy, when two become one, they still remain two. The Torah focuses on two becoming one in a physical sense ("and they shall be one flesh," Genesis 2:24); however, this does not include the merger of individual psyches. Even when two become one physically, in their psychological existence, each maintains his or her own thoughts and identities. They share these parts of themselves, to the extent that they want to, and when they deem this to be appropriate.

Each individual is also alone with his or her own image of God. This image constantly changes throughout one's life. Each person's relationship with God is unique. It is natural to be angry with God at times, just as it is natural to experience all types of feelings, from happiness to fear, in this relationship.

One is also alone with one's dreams and fantasies. In the moments before Jacob's encounter, he is alone, and a unique struggle then begins. That struggle has meaning and significance for the future -- for the Jewish people and humanity in general.

Jacob's struggle takes place during the night. The terms of the struggle are carefully delineated; it must end before the light of the next day, at dawn. The nighttime of the struggle is not meant to refer to the hours of darkness of that night. Rather, it could represent a period of darkness in the life of a person. That time period could be weeks, months or even years. No matter how much light that person is exposed to, this interval is his or her own nighttime.

A similar thought is expressed in the Passover *Haggadah*, in the famous question: "How is this night different from all other nights?" There are multifaceted interpretations of this central question of the Seder night. One interpretation suggests: "How is this exile different from other exiles that the Jewish people have experienced?"

The lonely night journey represents one's exile from one's self. When one is in this type of exile, it always feels like nighttime. One is engaged in a deep struggle, never knowing or anticipating the dawn of light and hope.

How does one feel in the midst of the darkness of exile? One is aware that the rest of the world is asleep, unaware of other people's plights, unaware of the agony and the sense of alienation being experienced by others. No *festive* meals or family gatherings ever take place during this lonely and dark time. One's only source of light during these moments is provided by looking heavenward, to the stars and the galaxies. However, contemplating the distance to those heavenly bodies only accentuates the sufferer's feelings of inadequacy, which can almost annihilate the individual. This period of nighttime seems never-ending, with no past and no future, only an eternal present of hopelessness and despair.

Equally deafening is the stillness of the night, in which almost all stimuli are diminished. At night, even if one is surrounded by noise, friends or conversation, one nevertheless sometimes feels so isolated as to be immune to external stimuli, since they seem to have no connection to the internal life. Ultimately, this lonely night journey represents the epitome of fear of the unknown -- of what is, what is to come, and what must be faced and learned about oneself.

"And a man (*Ish*) struggled with him." This "man" has no specific identity. This *Ish* without an identity is found only in a few other places in the entire Bible. One occurrence is in Genesis 18:2, where three "men" come to visit Abraham. Another is Genesis 37:15, where an *Ish* directs Joseph to where he can find his brothers. Another instance is in Exodus 2:12, where Moses, before he smites the Egyptian, looks around and sees that there is no *Ish*. Later on, in Judges 13:11, an *Ish* appears to Manoah and his wife, bearing news of the forthcoming birth of Samson.

In the case of Jacob's encounter, since the *Ish* has no specific identity, Biblical commentators throughout the ages have given the *Ish* various identities. Some say that he represents that which is externally hostile to Jacob, i.e., the image of Esau. Some commentators say that this *Ish* represents what is internally adverse to Jacob -- the dark, shadowy, trickster side of Jacob. And some commentators say that this *Ish* represents the dark image of God (Genesis *Rabbah* 77:3; Rashi and Rashbam on Genesis 32:25).

All three of these interpretations actually say the same thing, namely that Jacob was struggling with diverse aspects of himself. However, the Torah emphasizes that this encounter was with an *Ish*. This struggle could have been with another person, or with Jacob himself or with an angel of God taking the form of a human being. In one other place in the Bible, Judges 13:16, this *Ish* is identified as an angel of God. Another understanding of "angel of God" is "messenger of God." The messenger of God usually takes the form of a person.

I think that what the Torah wants to emphasize is a lesson for all generations to come. We also encounter angels of God throughout our lifetime. However, we do not always know who these persons may be. Perhaps they are those we would least expect to really help us or guide us. Therefore, we have to be specifically attuned to the unanticipated. We have to always be aware, knowing that a person we encounter may be representative of a divine message. This approach and attitude will naturally heighten our consciousness of every experience we have, every person crossing our path, every message and song we hear and every article we read.

II

Becoming One and Whole

What was Jacob's struggle? He was aware that perhaps he was facing his own mortality. He was aware that ultimately, justice might prevail. He was aware that lentil soup does not buy one the status of firstborn. He was aware that there was deception, even if preordained by divine prophecy to Rebeccah, in his receiving a blessing from his father.

He was aware that one cannot go on living a life of deception. He was aware that he wanted to make peace with his Creator.

The external threat of Jacob's meeting with his archenemy -- his brother, his twin -- revitalized the realization that before his possible death, he would want to be whole and at peace with himself. The possibility of his death was the catalyst for Jacob's internal struggle, the struggle of becoming one and whole, and of recognizing that one of the Patriarchs cannot build the Jewish people on a foundation of deceit that is ignored. Jacob was becoming increasingly conscious of the fact that what is ultimately required of each person is a metamorphosis and transformation as an individual human being.

No individual can ultimately rely on his or her lineage, even if that lineage includes Abraham and Isaac. No individual can ultimately rely on a mother, even if she is a Rebeccah, who receives private prophecy. No family situation and no circumstances of birth, childhood or young adulthood can be the determining factor of who one becomes. One cannot say: "I am the firstborn," or "I am the sandwich child," or "I am the last-born," and therefore attribute one's fate in life to birth order. Similarly, one cannot attribute one's destiny to having been favored by a mother or a father. Neither, for that matter, can one say that the future is determined by the constellation of stars at the time of birth, or by a famine endured in one's youth or by a Holocaust that one has survived.

Each person is ultimately responsible for what he or she becomes. Each person has to identify with his or her own struggle with Esau, i.e., one's dark side, or with shameful or embarrassing aspects of one's past. This struggle may take the form of a repetitive dream that has never been acted upon. A recurring dream may convey an important conceptual message, to which the dreamer has not listened or responded. Hopefully, during one's lifetime, while one is healthy, he or she will engage in a Jacob-like struggle of self-determination.

Jacob's struggle with Esau finds its analogue in contemporary life. Interestingly, Jacob's struggle was not initially metaphysical. At the outset, it was between him and his brother, his twin, so that it was a family struggle. Furthermore, it was a struggle that emanated from maternal nepotism in favor of Jacob and paternal nepotism in favor of Esau. This was almost a classic case of family enmeshment. Often I hear, both in my office and at patients' bedsides, the tremendous alienation, isolation and loneliness that people experience within the family context. Sometimes brothers and sisters have not spoken for years. Or, if they have spoken, there has been only speech from the mind, uttered politely, rather than words from the heart, spoken authentically.

Often I hear about a domineering mother and a weak father image or vice versa. This is one way that an adult-child constantly transfers the blame and fault for his or her own inadequacies in life. Frequently I hear how the umbilical cord has never been severed psychologically. Frequently the dissolution of a marriage is blamed on early childhood experiences, e.g., having a narcissistic mother or father. Frequently I am told that a person's struggles are due to abandonment by a mother or a father. Frequently I hear how "my father was an alcoholic and he abused me." Frequently I hear of all types of experiences that people use as justification for unhappiness, anxiety, fearfulness and impotence. Interestingly, these complaints that I hear from people in their thirties or forties are identical with the observations of people in their seventies, particularly among those who face imminent death. Jacob's struggle is a perennial struggle for each individual.

Darkness and Dawn

Jacob's struggle takes place during complete darkness. At the first arrival of light, the struggle automatically terminates. Is it not odd that while Jacob is in the midst of the struggle, he already knows when it will end? Jacob's struggle during the darkness epitomizes the dichotomy between one's public persona (meaning "mask") and one's private, individual struggles.

During daytime hours, people are well dressed and publicly polite; at times they may smile or laugh. They usually adapt to the appropriate social etiquette. During daytime hours, the emphasis is on social conformity and on not creating too many upheavals within the family or community unit. A person's professional title is the identification by which he or she is known. Habitual routines provide a sense of security and a predictable pattern of living. Nonconformity is usually perceived as an expression of boldness, assertiveness or aggressiveness.

But these daytime identities are masks that everyone wears. Every mask is dependent on the culture and society in which one is raised. However, all masks are removed in the darkness and stillness of the night. When one's public identity is removed, very fundamental and essential questions and struggles emerge, such as: "Who am I? Where am I going? How can I integrate my past with my present and my future? What is my destiny? Where is my personal God? What is my true experience of life and God, and who are my significant friends and family? What are my fears?"

Jacob, like everyone else, feels the enormous gap between his public life -- which seemingly even has the approval of divine providence -- and his innermost, internal struggle with life per se. The arrival of dawn not only coincides with the end of the struggle, but also perhaps represents a gradual integration of the public and the private individual. Perhaps the light is the first ray of the hope of redemption, where darkness and light can merge together. The darkness can shed meaning on the light and vice versa. Together, they constellate to create a new phenomenon called *the oneness and unity of life*.

Why did Jacob's struggle take place specifically in the darkness? What was his association with darkness? Jacob was constantly aware of how he had received the blessing of his father, thereby continuing in the tradition of Abraham and Isaac. Jacob was able to receive the blessing only because of Isaac's blindness, i.e., a form of nighttime. Isaac could feel and hear his son but could not see him.

For Jacob, the darkness on the night of the encounter with the *Ish* conjured up memories of how he had received his father's blessing by using deception. Jacob, the "whole person, dwelling in tents," had added darkness to his father's blindness. When one carries around memories such as this, the nighttime is inevitably unsettling.

What went through Jacob's mind regarding his father? Jacob may have said to himself: "How often I have heard that my father was a survivor of an attempted sacrifice. How often I have been told that his life was spared just as *his* father was about to sacrifice him on the altar. My father's life was saved literally by one second. Will I have the same fate? What will the *Ish* do to me? Will he turn into an angel and intercede for me as an angel did for my father, or will I be sacrificed on the altar of Yabok?

"Why did my father always have to remind me that he almost was sacrificed? I have grown up as a product of the second generation, fearful of being born and of surviving. I really am a 'whole person, dwelling in tents.' Did I start this struggle? No. The *Ish* initiated it. If the *Ish* represents a form of God in whatever guise, why is God struggling with man?

"The darkness is not complete, however. I am able to see a glimpse of the moon. There is some light. The *lunar* sphere is visible. I am reminded that perhaps I am a complete *lunatic*. So little light plunges me into more darkness. Perhaps I am imagining this whole thing, yet it hurts."

Things always look easier before they are attempted. In this case, the *Ish* initiated a fight and the *Ish* was the adversary. One would think that the *Ish* would only undertake such a mission if he felt he could prevail easily and quickly. There is always such a difference between observing life and living life. When one observes life and evaluates the pros and cons of a situation, one sometimes finds logical and rational solutions with great clarity. But in living life, the burdens of suffering, pain, grief, mourning and loss always overcome one with their intensity. The compassion and empathy of friends and family, as welcome as these qualities are, can never really overcome a person's private emotional experience.

I do not know whether this *Ish*'s initial plan was to kill Jacob -- to sacrifice him on the altar of Yabok -- or just to defeat him in a struggle. I do not know what is meant by "to be defeated in a struggle." Is it conceivable that the *Ish*, a divine messenger in human form, was attempting once again to have a human sacrifice, and this time he was actually accomplishing it himself? Was this God's struggle with Jacob, or with the divine Self? Does God need or want sacrifices, be they animal or human?

The *Ish* that Jacob encounters is known in Midrashic literature as either the "Prince of Jacob" or God Himself. Thus, he represents the most lofty and highest aspect of an individual who confronts the dark and shadow side of an individual. Why did this *Ish* begin a struggle with Jacob? Did he exhaust all of the other alternatives? Did he attempt a dialogue with

Jacob? Did he attempt softness, tenderness and love? Or, did this lofty and elevated *Ish* show his dark side by initially struggling and fighting with Jacob?

III

Esau and Jacob

Unable to physically prevail over Jacob, the *Ish* causes him an indelible disability, a permanent sign that will remain with Jacob for the rest of his life, causing him to limp. The hip joint connects the upper and lower parts of a person's body. An injury to that joint affects one's weight-bearing capabilities, so that Jacob's body weight is suddenly felt to be a burden every time he takes a step. There is a new image of Jacob limping. This is the outer expression of his weakness and vulnerability. His inner transformation, signified by his limping, is what makes possible Esau's reaction to him. Instead of attacking and killing Jacob, Esau is able to kiss him and to cry.

The Torah's statement, "and Esau kissed Jacob" (Genesis 33:4), is one of the ten places in the Torah where there are special markings within or above a word. Where the text reads "and he kissed him," there is a dot above each of the Hebrew letters. There is a beautiful Midrash (*Abot de Rabbi Natan*, Schechter ed., 51, 1, 6-49, 2) regarding this matter:

So said Ezra: "If Elijah comes and says to me, 'Why did you write in this manner?,' I will say to him: 'I have already placed dots on top [and therefore I cannot erase the words].' And if he says to me, 'How nicely this is written,' I will remove the dots from on top of the words.

What this Midrash expresses is that no matter how many generations pass, or how difficult it may be for people to understand this passage, the text regarding Esau's kissing Jacob will never be altered. In the encounter with Jacob, Esau takes the initiative in embracing Jacob. Esau is able to perceive the changed Jacob. Perhaps he even knows that Jacob's name is also Israel.

Another Midrash (*Sifre*, Numbers 69, Horowitz edition, p. 64) presents an alternate interpretation of the dots, suggesting that although Esau dislikes Jacob, he kisses him sincerely. The Midrash states:

> Rabbi Simeon bar Yohai says: "It is a well established principle that Esau [and that which is symbolized by him] dislikes Jacob. However, his emotions overwhelmed him and he kissed his brother with a full heart and sincerity."

The first Midrash anticipates the second one. Ezra has an intuition that despite the fact that the Torah says "and Esau kissed Jacob," later commentators may cast doubt on the authenticity and sincerity of this embrace and kiss.

The second Midrash is a fulfillment of the essential doubt concerning what is meant by the embrace and kiss. First, Esau's kissing is seen as ambivalent. Second, even if Esau's kissing is seen as sincere, one is cautioned from regarding Esau's and Jacob's behavior as a symbolic paradigm for the future of Gentile and Jewish relationships.

I, however, would like to believe that Ezra's interpretation contains the seeds of the Messianic ideal of the brotherhood of humanity. The message for eternity is that opposites and adversaries should be able to find unity despite their diverse outlooks. Hopefully, opposites can not only be tolerated, but also respected. Even when an irreconcilable clash emerges, the parties can respectfully agree to disagree.

As noted above, in Jacob's encounter with the *Ish*, he becomes changed both physically and psychologically. Jacob's limp is noticeable not just to him; it will always be visible to everyone else. Jacob will represent a living symbol of a most unusual struggle. During this struggle, does the *Ish* become hurt, or is he always on the offensive?

Furthermore, who is this *Ish*? If the *Ish* fighting with Jacob is a human being, this struggle can take place at night and continue into the daytime, as well. However, the description of the adversary as an *Ish* can be interpreted as a literary device to hint at the *Ish*'s true identity as an image of God. This strange power that initiates a struggle with Jacob functions specifically during the nighttime, so that the vast multitudes of people will not recognize this unusual aspect of the dark image of God.

This *Ish*, although he dislodges Jacob's hip, continues to struggle. When the struggle seems endless and the dawn approaches, the assailant quickly decides to present a polite aspect of himself, saying: "We will resume our struggle later, but right now we both need to resume our normal activities, because daytime is approaching."

Jacob is well aware of the treacherous power of the *Ish*. He remembers how, years before, he was foiled when, with all his heart and soul, he wanted to marry Rachel. During that other nighttime experience, Jacob was tricked into marrying Leah, rather than his beloved Rachel. Was it only his Uncle Laban who deceived Jacob? Or, was it through the atmosphere of darkness surrounding that evening that Jacob was somehow deceived? Jacob has learned to fear the nighttime, as a time when he can be deceived and when he sometimes loses control over what happens to him.

Blessing

During Jacob's encounter, he is aware that the *Ish* is capable of more than causing tremendous physical and psychological difficulties. Somehow, precisely because of these difficulties, Jacob can transform them into a blessing. It is at this juncture of the struggle, precisely at the first ray of dawn's light, that Jacob begins to have the upper hand in the struggle. Interestingly, Jacob does not want to take vengeance on the *Ish*. Rather, he desires a blessing from him.

What is a blessing? A blessing that one receives from God remains eternal. A blessing gives one guidance and support in multidimensional ways. A blessing (*berakhah*) adds humility to a person's character, since the root of the word relates to the knee and bending. The greatest blessing comes about when specifically, your adversary can bless you.

Apparently, the process of blessing begins when the adversary asks his opponent what his name is. At this point, Jacob feels completely startled. He knows that his grandfather's name was changed from Avram to Avraham (Genesis 17:5). He knows that his grandmother's name was changed from Sarai to Sarah (Genesis 17:15). And he realizes that the name changes of his grandparents were very significant. His grandfather became the Father of the multitude of nations. Not only the Israelites, but the Arabs, are descendents of Abraham. Furthermore, the name of his grandmother, Sarah, also indicates that she is a Matriarch for all. Both of his grandparents had their names changed to indicate a shift from the particular to the universal. Both in Biblical literature and in Aristotelian philosophy, the names of animals, plants and persons signify and designate the essence of the matter.

Jacob thinks: "Is my name going to be changed? I was not the firstborn. I am called 'Yaakov' (Jacob) because I held on to Esau's heel. Then I deceptively gained the rights of the firstborn. My name 'Yaakov' means 'trickster, supplanter,' indicating that I received the blessing from my father that was supposed to go to my brother, Esau. I have my own feelings about the significance of being firstborn. Can't every child be considered like a firstborn? Can't every child receive a coat of many colors? Can't the diamond of every child be discovered and polished? Can't ancestral blessings be bestowed on both children, Jacob and Esau, Isaac and Ishmael? Why does there have to be nepotism, creating a situation where certain children are excluded?"

By responding to the *Ish*, "my name is Jacob," Jacob admits that his past includes very dark and deceptive parts of his life. At the same moment, he is aware that perhaps his Uncle Laban's tricking him into marrying Leah was punishment for Jacob's own deception. Jacob realizes that the foundation of the Jewish people will never endure without coming to terms with who Jacob is and what he did to secure the ancestral blessings. Jacob is aware that what he perpetrated in deceiving Esau and Isaac was the heinous crime of psychological betrayal.

The blessing that Jacob receives takes the form of Jacob's being given an additional name, a new identity. No longer will Jacob constantly feel guilty, trying to wash the blood of deception from his hands. He will be able to stand erect, proud of who he is and who he was, a man guided by a mysterious divine force and one who has become a progenitor of the Jewish people.

However, Jacob is somewhat unsure of what the name "Israel" means. He initially thinks that he is connected to his grandmother, Sarai, as he becomes the "Sar El," the Prince of God. But his doubts are resolved when the *Ish* elaborates on the exact meaning of his new name and identity of Israel.

The *Ish*'s explanation to Jacob, "that you have prevailed with God and with men," gives Jacob courage in approaching his brother, Esau. Jacob has a visceral feeling that this lonely night journey will serve him well. However, the name "Israel" has an even more profound meaning for Jacob. Not only does he feel comforted concerning his future encounter with Esau, but also he feels that his honest encounter with the *Ish* allowed him to do battle with God, leaving him limping, yet victorious.

Jacob now has a new realization of the multiple images of God. One past image was quite beautiful for him, when he had his dream (Genesis 28) about the Ladder of Ascension. There, the angels of God were seen ascending and descending, and they promised Jacob that God would always be with him and his descendents. But, in this case, Jacob has another image of God. This time, He is seen in the form of an *Ish*, who initiates struggles with individuals. Jacob is therefore able to have a composite picture of the divine. Consequently, he does not have to ask the perennial questions, "Why me? Why now?" Jacob realizes that God is present in the beauty of life, but also in the struggles of life.

Jacob is also aware that his name is not only Israel, but also Jacob. This realization is that which is echoed by King David, in Psalms (51:5): "My sin, my history, who I am can always be transcended, but can never be eliminated." Jacob realizes that, "I am Israel, and I have prevailed with God and with men [both Esau and Laban], but I am also Jacob. These multiple identities will be with me throughout my life."

Jacob's question regarding the *Ish*'s name is quite different from the question the *Ish* put to him. Jacob structures his sentence politely and uses the word *na*, "please," though the *Ish* used no niceties. Why does Jacob want to know the *Ish*'s name? Is this a matter of cordial reciprocity? Or, does Jacob audaciously plan to bless the *Ish* by giving him an additional name?

Jacob is certainly to be commended for having the forbearance and presence of mind in this encounter to ask for the *Ish*'s name. At this point, is Jacob foreshadowing Moses' request to know the Name of God (Exodus 3:14)? When Moses asks for God's Name, God tells him that "I am that I am." That is, the image of God will continuously change for each individual throughout his or her lifetime.

When Jacob asks for the name of the *Ish*, he is rebuked by that divine messenger, who responds: "Why are you asking for my Name?" As previously indicated, this *Ish* appears numerous times in the Bible, but nowhere is his true identity revealed. However, upon closer scrutiny, it may be that his lack of identity represents the same truth that was revealed to Moses, i.e., " I am that I am." In one instance, the *Ish* appears to Jacob as an adversary. However, this same *Ish* appears to Joseph and directs him to his brothers. And the *Anashim* (a plural form of *Ish*) who come to visit Abraham have multiple identities. So perhaps the *Ish*'s identity is, in fact, "I am that I am."

I am puzzled by the *Ish*'s blessing Jacob at the conclusion of their encounter (Genesis 32:30). I thought that the blessing had already taken place through Jacob's name being changed to Israel. Yet, I doubt that this latter blessing is a recapitulation of the first one. I hypothesize that after changing Jacob's name and speaking with Jacob about his own concealed name, the *Ish* gave Jacob an additional blessing, whose contents are not revealed to us. However, I would like to speculate about the content of this blessing. Jacob wanted to know the identity of this *Ish*. Jacob wanted and needed support, not a physical cane to support his limping leg, but rather a spiritual cane that would allow Jacob to derive everlasting meaning from God's struggle with him. In this second blessing, he received an eternal spiritual blessing.

IV

Experiencing the Divine

Jacob designated the name of the place of the encounter as "Peniel," acknowledging that he had been privileged to see God face to face. He further acknowledged that in this process, his life had been spared.

In order to understand this central sentence relating to Jacob's perception of the whole struggle, it is necessary to examine Exodus 33, sentences 17 through 23. After the episode of the Golden Calf and the breaking of the first Tablets of the Law, Moses asks to have the unique privilege of understanding the honor of God. God reveals to Moses His moral attributes of mercy and compassion. But He says that the ultimate understanding of God shall remain unfathomable to Moses and to every other mortal. He tells Moses that "you will be able to understand My back, but the essence of who I am, represented by My *face*, shall remain impenetrable." Thus, what God says to Moses is that despite all human strivings -- of intellect, emotion and spirit -- there shall always remain a partial eclipse of God.

Moses, as the greatest of the Prophets, *knew* God *"face to face"* (Exodus 33:11, Deuteronomy 34:10 and Numbers 12:8). These citations, however, merely describe the status of Moses' prophecy, indicating how it differed from that of the other Prophets. Moses' prophecy was more intimate and more direct, although even he was not allowed to see the face of God.

Indeed, one of the thirteen Principles of Faith, recited daily, is the declaration of the uniqueness of Moses' prophecy. Biblical commentators are, therefore, very troubled in explaining Jacob's actually seeing God face to face. The *Targum Onkelos* tries to reconcile this contradiction by saying that Jacob saw the face of the angel, but not of God.

When it comes to a request for the cognitive understanding of God, such as that put forth by Moses, one cannot obtain a satisfactory response, i.e., cognition of a divine Being. However, Jacob's request was not cognitive. He was describing his *experience* of struggling with the darkness of God Himself.

The distinction between cognition and experience is essential. While cognition refers to an epistemological comprehension of God, which is *ipso facto* limited, an experience, of necessity, allows one to come to various images of God. That is why everyone's life journey is unique, singular and incomparable to anyone else's life journey.

The experience of life is unique to each individual. Each person has his or her own mode of thinking and reflecting, conscious and unconscious thoughts, complexities of the psyche, fantasies and dreams. Only through subjectivity in defining the essence of the human being, can one say: "I have been privileged to see the face of God in totality." The seemingly unbridgeable gap between humanity and divinity can be overcome only through a deepening of one's self, as one struggles with the multiple images of God in one's life.

Varying images of God are recounted throughout the Biblical narrative. Moses uses a very strong and unique image of the divine in his Song of Gratitude after crossing the Sea of Reeds. In one verse (Exodus 15:3), composed after Moses and the Israelites witness the miraculous hand of God in the initial redemptive process, Moses declares that God is an *Ish* of War. This is the sole Biblical reference to God as an *Ish*. Perhaps this is similar to the image of God that initiated the struggle with Jacob. The statement that God is not an *Ish* (Numbers 23:19) does not negate the aforementioned.

The Jacob in Us

The Bible does not tell us that the sun rose, but that it rose "for him," i.e., for Jacob. It rose for someone who had become Israel, who had received an unknown blessing and who had been privileged to see God face to face.

There is tremendous risk in exploring the unknown. The Talmud recounts the mystical explorations of four great Sages who wanted to discover the secrets of life (*Hagigah* 14b). Of these four, only Rabbi Akiba emerged peacefully. Ben Azzai looked too deeply and died; Ben Zoma looked too deeply and became demented; and Aher became an apostate.

However, other explorations are often regarded as essential to undertake. People often perceive danger in struggling with life and with God, yet each individual needs to examine these aspects of life.

Maimonides (*Mishneh Torah, Hilkhot Yesodei ha-Torah* 4:13) has an interesting suggestion in terms of one's development and growth. He states that before one undertakes an exploration of the mysteries of life, one should achieve external stability. The Talmud (*Sukkah* 28a) defines this achievement as having studied all of the questions of Abbaye and Rava regarding how one should conduct oneself in daily behavior and routine.

Both Maimonides and the Talmud suggest that the exploration of life should begin when one is approximately at mid-life, or what C. G. Jung refers to as the beginning of the second half of life. Jacob's encounter with the *Ish* constituted his mid-life journey. What happened to Jacob, when the sun shone for him, was the conceptual antecedent of Rabbi Akiba's experience. Jacob explored life in depth and became lame, yet the sun shone for him.

Avram's name was changed permanently to Avraham. Likewise, Sarai's name was changed permanently to Sarah. Only Jacob was given an *alternate* name, Israel. In the Book of Genesis, the names Jacob and Israel are frequently used interchangeably. These references indicate that there is a balance in life between opposing forces, such as light and darkness, or good and evil. Even though the sun shone for Jacob, the sun always sets; the sun does not shine permanently for anyone.

The text indicates that the sun shone for Jacob as he passed Peniel. The emphasis here is on the past tense. From this choice of verb, we learn that there is a difference between the moment something is experienced and the moments that follow. At the height of an experience, there may be confusion, or even chaos. Additional time is needed to integrate the new experience with one's prior knowledge.

Piaget refers to new, cognitive knowledge that needs to be integrated as the process of accommodation. What Jacob needed to do was to recognize that God can struggle with human beings. Both divinity and humanity can become victors; they both can become Israel.

In Jacob's encounter, the *Ish* was not defeated. A new image of God appeared to Jacob. Therefore, we can say that the image of God became enhanced for Jacob.

As mentioned above, Jacob's injury is visible to all. We, as the descendents of Jacob and the Children of Israel, have inherited his limp. For us, this limp represents the complexity of what it means to be human and Jewish and what it means to have an ever-changing relationship with God.

The Hebrew word used in the text for "limped" is *tzolea*. Through word association, one is reminded of the birth of Eve, the first woman. This birthing process (Genesis 2:21-22) is carried out using the *tzela* ("side" or "rib") of Adam. God's removal of Adam's rib is symbolic of a rebirth. Henceforth, there will be both man and woman.

In the creation story, Adam receives as a companion a woman (*Isha*) who is fashioned from his *tzela*. Similarly, the limping Jacob will forever be accompanied by Israel. Now, while Jacob limps, it will always be possible for each individual to struggle with God and see Him face to face.

The Thigh-Vein

Because the *Ish* dislodged the hollow of Jacob's thigh, the Children of Israel are prohibited forever from eating the sinew of the thigh-vein. This is the first Biblical reference to the Jewish people as the "Children of Israel." From this source, we learn that the first thing to remember, and remember eternally, is that we are the descendents of Jacob, but we need to become the Children of Israel.

Only three commandments to the Jewish people appear in the Book of Genesis, the Book that represents the foundation of the Torah, the Jewish people and humanity. The first commandment is to be fruitful and multiply in order to sustain the world. The second requires that all Jewish males undergo ritual circumcision, which constitutes a special covenant between God and the Jewish people. The third, and the first prohibition in the Torah, is the commandment that proscribes eating the sinew of the thigh-vein.

This commandment must be equal in importance to the other two commandments in Genesis. I suggest that this first prohibition serves as a constant reminder that Jacob's limp, and his transformation from Jacob into Israel, serves as a paradigm for each Jew. Through it, we are reminded that each of us has to go through a lonely night journey in becoming who we are destined to be.

V

The Lonely Night Journey

Jacob's remaining alone and then going through the experience of his encounter is variously described as "the dark night of the soul," "the night sea journey," or "the hero's quest," a voyage which all must travel if they are driven toward the goal of realizing their creative potential.

Moses went through a similar journey. In the Book of Exodus, after accepting the mission to be the leader of the Jewish people, and after experiencing the numinosity of the Burning Bush, Moses has an encounter "*on the way*, at the lodging place" (Exodus 4:24). God appears to Moses, seeking to kill him because he has not circumcised his son. Moses' wife, Zipporah, saves his life, yet Moses experiences a "dark night of the soul." Here is a man who on one day is appointed leader of the Jewish people by God Himself, yet on the next day, experiences the possibility of his imminent death at the hand of God.

Jacob's experience and Moses' experience accentuate the fact that opposing forces of creative energy need to be recognized. Jacob feared the "Esau" energy, and Moses, a male, needed to recognize the feminine energy expressed by his wife, Zipporah.

Every person, in traveling along the journey of life, exposed to the hardships of life and the world, must depart from his or her family and from assorted collective traditions, as well as from self-imposed limitations. This journey requires courage. It ultimately allows everyone to live life to the fullest.

At the end of Jacob's life, as he bestows his paternal blessing on all of his children who will become the Twelve Tribes of Israel, he gathers them around his deathbed (Genesis 49:1-33). He seeks reassurance that the values of his grandfather and father, as well as his own values, will be carried on for generations to come.

Jacob wants the comfort of knowing that the Twelve Tribes of Israel will always be imbued with the covenantal promise. In unison, the sons, forming a circle around their father's bed, proclaim: "Hear, O Israel, the

Eternal our God: the Eternal is the Unique One." And when they say, "Hear, O Israel," their reference is not to the collective people of Israel, but to Jacob, their father.

Just before Jacob hears these reassuring words, he eloquently states that two of his grandchildren, Ephraim and Manasseh, the two sons of Joseph, are as dear to him as his own sons, Reuben and Simeon (Genesis 48:5). Indeed, Ephraim and Manasseh become part of the Twelve Tribes; the tribe of Joseph is represented by his two sons.

It is very puzzling that Joseph, who was the most beloved son of Jacob, as well as the son of his old age, suddenly recedes from the picture of the Twelve Tribes, replaced by his two sons, Ephraim and Manasseh. Furthermore, it has become traditional in Jewish homes, on Friday night and the eve of holidays, to bless one's children by saying, "May God make you like Ephraim and Manasseh."

Why were Jacob's grandchildren selected as an eternal blessing for all generations to come? I suggest that when a Jew recites the "Hear, O Israel" daily, or blesses a child before the Sabbath or a holiday, something symbolic is occurring. What is being represented is the fact that we are all reciting "Hear, O Israel," referring to Jacob, our father. We, who are separated from him by approximately 3,000 years, reaffirm the principle that "the Eternal, our God, the Eternal is the Unique One," thereby bridging time. We say to Jacob: "We have also *become* your children."

This understanding explains why we are known as the Children of Israel, i.e., the children of Jacob. We respond as the children of Jacob did, reaffirming the Jewish declaration of faith, "Hear, O Israel, the Eternal, our God: the Eternal is the Unique One."

The Talmud (*Taanit* 5b) states that "Jacob, our father, has not died." In emphasizing the eternal spirit of our forefather, the Talmud selects the name "Jacob," and not "Israel." Furthermore, the Talmud stresses the fact that Jacob *our father* has not died.

We all must strive to see ourselves as the children of Jacob at some point in our lives, identifying with his struggles as well as our own. Then, each of us can become an "Israel." The transformation of Jacob into Israel serves as a model for each of us. First, we recognize that "Jacob, our father, has not died." And then, we can each say, "Hear, O Israel, the Eternal, our God: the Eternal is the Unique One."

PART III

CONCLUSION

CHAPTER VII

REFLECTIONS ON THE DEATH OF MY ANALYST

When I entered into Jungian analysis with Dr. James Kirsch, who was then 84 years old, I had a premonition that my analyst might die during the period of my analysis. Nevertheless, I decided to enter into this "everlasting relationship." What were my conscious and unconscious motivations for this decision? Consciously, Dr. Kirsch represented to me the archetype of the wise old man, someone who had integrated the wisdom of the heart and the experience of life with universal knowledge, especially the heritage of the Jewish tradition. His library was as diverse as it was comprehensive. Naturally, it included many books on psychoanalysis and analytical psychology, the classics in German, English, and American literature, and in social anthropology; but it also included comprehensive works on the Bible, Talmud, *Kabbalistic* (Jewish mystical), and *Hassidic* (Jewish pietistic) literature. He also had a very rare and early edition of the complete writings of William Shakespeare.

I was aware that Dr. Kirsch was the last Los Angeleno "Joshua" of the Jungian tradition, having maintained contact with Carl Gustav Jung from 1928 until Jung's death in 1961. I would be a part of the link in the tradition and become an "elder" (Mishnah, *Avot* 1:1). The connection to the source would be direct. Many of the prominent thinkers and scientists of the 19th and 20th centuries did, in fact, become real for me during the process of my analysis. Indeed, Sigmund Freud, Carl Gustav Jung, Albert Einstein, Martin Buber and others became significant visitors to my dreams during this period. They all had entered my unconscious. The dream-pictures I had of these people were strikingly similar to their actual appearances. I was receiving a living oral tradition.

I met Dr. James Kirsch a year before I started my analysis with him. He invited me to teach him the classic Jewish interpretations of dreams in the Book of Genesis, and he offered to share with me Jungian interpretations of the same dreams. I was his teacher and he was mine at the same time.

Unconsciously, perhaps I selected James Kirsch because I desired to learn more about the dying process and of death itself from my analyst. I would *experience* his dying process with him. I knew that only his death -- not any prior termination on my part -- would terminate the analysis.

When our analytic relationship began, he shared with me the fact that I was the first Rabbi to become his analysand. I found it quite unusual that he shared this information with me. I thought that he had an inkling that my presence at this time in his life had a very special meaning for his life and primarily, for his death.

This "analyst-Rabbi" relationship was unusual from a different perspective, as well. In 1973, Dr. Kirsch had authored a remarkable book entitled *The Reluctant Prophet: An Exploration of Prophecy and Dreams*, explaining the dreams of Rabbi Hile Wechsler, an Orthodox Rabbi in a small Bavarian town. In 1881, Wechsler's dreams foretold an impending catastrophe that could be compared only with Noah's Flood -- the forthcoming Holocaust in Europe. Thus, the first "analyst-Rabbi" relationship had an equally profound meaning for both the analyst and the analysand.

Throughout our analytic relationship, Dr. Kirsch presented himself in various roles, each one appropriate to the individual issues I raised. When I presented issues of a personal, medical nature, he assumed the role of a psychiatrist. My dreams were interpreted by a Jungian analyst, and my interpersonal behaviors were facilitated by a caring and sensitive psychologist.

Dr. Kirsch's most important role, however, was that of a spiritual father and *Rebbe* (personal spiritual mentor). Although I had received a very comprehensive Jewish education at Yeshiva Rabbi Samson Raphael Hirsch and Yeshiva University in New York -- two schools that accentuate the integration of religious development with Western civilization -- I discovered my *Rebbe* and spiritual guide in my analyst, Dr. James Kirsch. Interestingly, he was visibly honored and graciously accepted his new title of *Rebbe*.

The motto of Yeshiva Rabbi Samson Raphael Hirsch is *Torah im Derekh Eretz*, which represents the integration of a religious life with secular professions. The motto of Yeshiva University is *Torah u-Mada*, which epitomizes the unity of religious life and scientific knowledge. Both schools strive for the unity and integration of diverse aspects of life.

James Kirsch did not see the world or life as composed of the sacred and the secular. In his world view, everything has sparks of holiness and Divinity. The reality of a living God was paramount to Dr. Kirsch. For him, one example of this reality was his interpretation of the Jewish prayer, which we recited together a few days before he died. While our hands were clasped together, we prayed the *Shema Yisroel* (Deuteronomy 6:4, "Hear, O Israel; the Eternal, Our God: the Eternal is the Unique One"), the Jewish declaration of faith. Dr. Kirsch explained that the oneness of God with humanity is not only in the hereafter, but also throughout one's life. The years which we are granted are part of the overall spiritual eternity.

This spirituality was also present in all of Dr. Kirsch's activities. With reverence and reticence, I share a very personal moment that took place a week before he died. While lying in bed in a very weakened condition, he asked me to feed him some papaya. He ate the papaya with enthusiasm and zest for life. He loved what he was doing. He realized how nutritious this fruit was for him. He ate the papaya with dignity. He had completely sacrificed his ego, and he felt holy and pure as he was being fed. I felt immensely privileged that I was given that opportunity.

James's process of individuation was genuinely lifelong. He articulated and practiced what he believed. In July 1988, James had planned to visit Carl Alfred Meier, M.D., in Zurich, Switzerland, to continue their lifelong talks face-to-face. James told me that Carl Alfred Meier's quiet presence was very powerful and would constellate for James a deepening of his psyche. Unfortunately, just prior to the date of his proposed departure, James fell and was hospitalized. He made a remarkable recovery.

Although the meeting with Meier never took place, the proposed event had synchronistic meaning for me. Carl Alfred Meier, the founder of the C.G. Jung Institute in Zurich, was James's lifelong friend and mentor. Upon Jung's retirement in 1949, Dr. Meier succeeded him as Professor at the Swiss Federal Institute. My father's name is Alfred Meier, and my great-grandfather's name is Carl Meier. These "coincidences" had a very profound and symbolic value for me. My analyst was indeed my spiritual father and *Rebbe*. There were other similarities as well. Both James and I had written chapters (that appeared consecutively) in *A Modern Jew in Search of a Soul* (Spiegelman and Jacobson, 1986); and we were both members of the editorial board of *The Journal of Psychology and Judaism* (1981-89).

In my frequent visits to James towards the end of his life, he was lying in bed in a very weakened state. At times he would doze off and then slightly reawaken. I asked him what he had been thinking. He replied, "In my life I have been lucky and unlucky." He commented further that his association with Carl Gustav Jung was his good fortune. "Jung," he added, "was a man of the millennium, a man of the millennium. The unluckiness was the experience of the Holocaust."

When during our analytic sessions he discovered that I frequently officiate at funerals, he asked me to officiate at his funeral. I was honored, nervous and overwhelmed by the request, and I said "yes" in a soft tone.

James was particularly sensitive and careful that most of our analytical sessions would focus on my issues and dreams. During one of our sessions, however, James wanted to initiate our discussions. Intuitively, I switched from analysand to Rabbi, friend and colleague. James had just received a transatlantic telephone call, informing him that Dr. Gerhard Adler of London had just died. He shared that news with me. After briefly reminiscing about his relationship with Gerhard Adler, he asked me whether I had heard about the recent death of his other lifelong friend, Dr. Ernst Simon. Both of these individuals were very close to James and contributors to a *Festschrift* in his honor (1971). Their deaths put James in a reflective mood.

That same day, December 23, 1988, was also the secular *Yahrzeit* for his wife, Hilde, who had died on December 23, 1978. James told me that he never anticipated that he would survive those ten additional years. "As a matter of fact," he added, "I think I will die this year." On that day in 1988, James was dressed somewhat more formally than was his custom. He told me that he was going to visit his wife's grave in Eden Memorial Park.

I experienced that day's session very powerfully, to such an extent that Hilde Kirsch visited me in my dreams a few days later. She represented an aspect of my anima, and I felt privileged to have had an unconscious relationship with her.

Dr. James Kirsch was blessed with five children. One of them was unable to attend the funeral service, since he resides in London. At the funeral, as the coffin was being lowered, I assisted the four children present in their tearing *Keriah*, a rending of the garment to symbolize the utter ineffableness of this moment of anguish. Words were insufficient. Silence was deafening. The act of *Keriah* was performed with tears and in a solemn atmosphere. After reciting the appropriate blessing with each of his children, while rending each of their garments, I was asked to rend one more garment for his son in London who was unable to be there at that moment. With tears in my eyes, *I* tore *Keriah*, not only for his son in London, but also for my own spiritual father and *Rebbe*.

Our analytical sessions were fascinating to me. He had personal contact with many significant 20th-century thinkers and scientists. He met Freud on two occasions and referred to Sigmund Freud as a tremendous pioneer in the discovery of the unconscious and of the central role that it plays. He called Freud a *Maggid*, a *Hassidic* term referring to a good story-teller. He met Albert Einstein and marveled at his genius -- but also took note of his lack of reality function. Once, at a banquet, Einstein was sitting at the dais, where a special flower had been placed in front of each plate for esthetics and decor. Einstein began to munch on the flower. Immediately a poison control center was called; the flower was not toxic. While all this was going on, the other guests at the banquet started to munch on their flowers, thinking that if Einstein thought them edible, they definitely were so. Fascinating stories and anecdotes ensued, referring to Martin Buber, Franz Rosenzweig and Abraham Joshua Heschel. James referred to Jung as one of the most spiritual people ever to live. He talked a little about Jung's secret "Red Book" that would be available only 30 years after Jung's death, something he intuitively knew he would not have access to.

When James Kirsch reached the age of 84 years, he wrote an autobiographical essay (Spiegelman and Jacobson, 1986) that was very revealing and significant. At the age of 13, James Kirsch walked alone through a little wood. Suddenly, he heard a voice speaking very clearly to him: "You shall become like Abraham and Moses and found a new people" (p. 149). This occurrence he had shared with Jung and with no one else until the writing of that essay at the age of 84 years. As a result of this communication, James felt he had experienced a numinous event and had a direct connection with God. God's continuing revelation to man had taken place and was able to take place with everyone as "information continues to come from the unconscious into the conscious" (p. 152). Rabbinically, Abraham is referred to as Abraham, our *father*, and Moses is referred to as Moses, our *teacher*. As an analyst, James Kirsch was indeed a father and *Rebbe*, as he introduced his own family and many others to Jungian psychology.

At the conclusion of the funeral service, a special memorial prayer was recited in memory of James's wife, Hilde, and his lifelong friend, Max Zeller, who together with Lore Zeller were the co-founders of the Jungian groups in Los Angeles. With that prayer, the funeral service was concluded, and people greeted and comforted one another.

As I returned to the car with James's son, Tom, we both looked back and noticed that hardly anyone had left the burial site. This behavior was unusual. Different thoughts crossed my mind, until I settled on the ancient Rabbinic maxim about Jacob, our patriarch. It states that *Yaakov Avinu Lo Met* (Talmud, *Taanit* 5b), Jacob, our father, has not died. This statement refers to the spiritual legacy that a father bequeaths to his heirs. I can say that James Kirsch, our spiritual father, has not died. His spiritual legacy continues forever.

One aspect of his spiritual legacy that left an indelible impression on me was his ability to recognize his disabilities, yet at the same time not allow those aspects of his life to transform him into a disabled person. Our analytic sessions began in a slow manner. He used either my hand or his cane as an aid in descending a flight of stairs, and then he used a walker to reach the room where our sessions took place. Once seated, he would insert his hearing aids and begin with a beautiful and warm welcome in Hebrew, "*Boker Tov*, Levi" (Good Morning, Levi). He usually needed to utilize the bathroom once during each of our sessions. These occasions were never considered to be interruptions. The uplifting manner in which he verbalized what he was doing was a song to the listener. He used all the disabilities that befell him toward the end of his lifetime, knowingly and unknowingly, as teaching models for all who came into contact with him.

He never forgot anyone who came into his life. A few weeks before he died, while he could barely talk for any length of time, he shared with me the fact that he was thinking of all the people who had not completed their work with him. He analyzed himself to determine if he had done anything that would have precipitated a premature termination on the part of the analysand. He hoped and prayed that they all had continued along their inner paths.

A few weeks before James died, my wife and I visited him. I had wanted my wife, Marcie, to meet with James. He greeted Marcie from his bed, "Good morning, Marcie, mother of four children." James, in his weakened state, engaged Marcie in friendly and erudite conversation. They discussed the Hebrew word *Tehom* ("depth," Genesis 1:2) and its etymological relationship to the name of the Babylonian goddess, *Tiamat*. They also discussed people they knew in common, including Rabbi F.E. Rottenberg of Los Angeles, who had once invited Dr. James and Hilde to participate in a Passover Seder. (Rabbi Rottenberg contributed a special appendix on *Gematria* [numerology] and *Kabbalah* to Dr. Kirsch's book on Rabbi Wechsler.) We all enjoyed this visit immensely. James turned to me and said, "Your wife is a very well-educated woman."

James put a lot of emphasis on synchronistic events as guides and omens. The Hebrew day of his death had a symbolic meaning for me. He died, at the age of 87, on a Sabbath (Friday, March 17, 1989 at 8:40 p.m., corresponding to the 11th day of Adar II, 5749), on which the reading of the *Torah* began with the word *VaYikra* ("And He called unto Moses," Leviticus 1:1). What was engraved on Jung's door, "Summoned or not, God is always present," was also true for James Kirsch on the day that God selected to call him.

James's first numinous experience, when he heard God's voice call to him at the tender age of 13, began with the statement: "You shall become like Abraham and Moses and found a new people" (Spiegelman and Jacobson, 1986, p. 149). God gave James Kirsch numerous roles and different names (his Hebrew name was *Yitzchak*), one of them being Moses. And on that day, *VaYikra*, God called unto this new Moses. Even in his death, Dr. Kirsch was called by God. This calling was even visible at the moment of death. In eulogizing Kirsch, his son Tom stated:

And I came down from San Francisco and, ten minutes after I was there, he died. And I looked at him and I looked at the expression on his face, and there was such a peace, and he looked so radiant and in a way so youthful, that it really gave me such a sense of satisfaction that there must have been something that had gone right in his life to have him look like that at the end.

James was particularly pleased to know that some newborn babies had been given the name James in his honor. I think this happiness was twofold. These namings represented a sense of continuity. But they meant more than that. These namings symbolized the love of many, many people -- friends and family members -- who had surrounded James in his lifetime. At the funeral, one of his grandchildren, Debbie, beautifully summarized these loving feelings by sharing the following:

> Grandpa, as James was known to all of us grandchildren, was, if there is such a thing, the perfect archetypal grandfather. He was a stable and loving force in our lives. There are so many memories. Our memories are so strong of Sunday lunches with him and Grandma and assorted other family members gathered around the table with chicken and red cabbage and marinated cucumbers or tomatoes. Hanukahs were always a special family time, as everyone would dart from family group to family group to view the presents and suck up the good feelings that always filled the living room. My sister Judy recalls teaching Grandpa how to blow bubbles with chewing gum and that he used to pay her ten cents for a swimming lesson. He would hide her shoes when she took them off to play in the house, a fact discovered only when it was time to leave... Being James Kirsch's granddaughter may have given me an unearned feeling of inflated self-importance. For as long as I can remember, people responded to us with awe and respect when our status as grandchildren of James Kirsch was known.

> I knew he was important to a lot of people and for a lot of reasons that I didn't really understand. But, more significantly, he was important to us, and I am sure he was to his other grandchildren as well, because he made us laugh and took us on fun vacations, and he was the loving and adoring grandfather any young child could hope for.

A *Festschrift* (1971) was presented to James Kirsch on the occasion of his 70th birthday by his friends and colleagues from London, Zurich, Berlin, New York, Jerusalem and Los Angeles. It is a beautiful volume and a magnificent expression of the love and affection which all the contributors expressed to James. The title of the book, *The Well-Tended Tree*, encompasses and epitomizes the essence of James Kirsch. James Kirsch represents the Tree of Life. A tree has roots that are solid and well grounded, a trunk that stands tall and erect, and branches and leaves. James symbolized the roots for so many people and in that way, he was the beginning of a new Tree of Life. The branches are "You shall become like Abraham and Moses and found a new people." The different shapes and contours of the leaves are many different types of people from different cultures and religions who all found their inspiration in James Kirsch. He genuinely appreciated the viewpoints and backgrounds of other people. He was a physician to Jews, Christians, Taoists, Muslims, Buddhists and others. In all these ways, James Kirsch symbolized the Tree of Life.

This universal message of the Tree of Life was personally conveyed to me when I asked James, "What would you like me to say at your funeral?" He responded with two items. "Let people know that I, James Kirsch, am very proud to be a Jew, and as a Jew and through my collective unconscious, I am open to the universal message of the great Prophets."

The second item, which he said with a smile, was "Whatever else you say, don't speak too long at my funeral." I feel James's spirit to be with me very much even now -- so I will not write too much either, as he wished.

At the funeral service, another of his sons, James Silver, read a short passage from the Book of Ways:

The master gives himself up to whatever the moment brings. He knows that he is going to die and he has nothing left to hold onto; no illusions in his mind, no resistances in his body. He doesn't think about his actions. They flow from the core of his being. He holds nothing back from life. Therefore he is ready for death as a man is ready for sleep after a good day's work.

Yaakov Avinu Lo Met (Talmud, *Taanit* 5b) -- Jacob, our father, has not died. *Kol Yaakov Hai* -- the voice of Jacob, the voice of James -- resonates forever.

References

Kirsch, H. (Ed.). (1971). *The well-tended tree: Essays into the spirit of our time.* New York: G.P. Putnam's Sons for the C.G. Jung Foundation for Analytical Psychology.

Kirsch, J. (1973). *The reluctant prophet: An explanation of prophecy and dreams.* Los Angeles: Sherbourne Press, Inc.

Spiegelman, J.M. and Jacobson, A. (Eds.). (1986). *A modern Jew in search of a soul.* Phoenix, Arizona: Falcon Press.

The Talmud. (18 vols.) (1961). I. Epstein (Ed.). London: Soncino Press.

CHAPTER VIII

BOOK REVIEW

**Freud and Moses: The Long Journey Home,
by Emanuel Rice. Albany, New York,
State University of New York Press, 1990. 266 pages.**

Freud and Moses: The Long Journey Home presents an insightful, penetrating and brilliant alternative view of Sigmund Freud (1856-1939), one markedly different from that of Peter Gay's *A Godless Jew: Freud, Atheism and the Making of Psychoanalysis* or Ernest Jones' *The Life and Work of Sigmund Freud.*

Dr. Emanuel Rice, a practicing psychiatrist and professor of psychiatry at the Mount Sinai School of Medicine of the City University of New York, has carefully examined almost all of Freud's writings and correspondence, including anecdotal and previously unpublished information. The only material that he does not examine is the correspondence between Sabina Spielrein, Jung and Freud; those writings, discovered in 1977, in fact provide additional support for Rice's thesis. Rice maintains that there is a dichotomy between Freud's public disassociation from God, religion and ritual and his internal religious conflicts. According to Rice, Freud resolved this dualism by his "long journey home," determining that his life's work had indeed been concerned with the essence of Judaism, i.e., the unconscious and all of its manifestations. Rice succeeds in providing new perspectives on the life of Sigmund Freud and the relationship between psychoanalysis and religion, in general, and psychoanalysis and Judaism, in particular.

In the preface to the Hebrew edition of his *Totem and Taboo* (1930), Freud, referring to himself in the third person, wrote:

If the question were put to him: "Since you have abandoned all these common characteristics of your countrymen, what is there left to you that is Jewish?" he would reply: "A great deal, and probably its very essence."

It was during Freud's adolescence that he demonstrated rebelliousness toward his Jewish identity as he changed his name from Shlomo Sigismund Freud to Sigmund Freud. Nevertheless, this adolescent phase eventually gave way to a more positive Jewish identity. Freud became a member of B'nai Brith (1897), acquired a complete set of the Talmud, in both the original language and translation, and was appointed to the Board of Governors of Hebrew University in Jerusalem (1925), demonstrating his Zionist tendencies.

Contrary to the popular view of Freud's parents as assimilated Jews, Rice effectively argues that both came from Orthodox Jewish families and continued to uphold many traditions. For example, date notations made by Sigmund's father, Jacob (1815-1896), in the family Bible indicate that he did not want to recognize the Christian calendar, in accordance with a custom prevalent among Orthodox Jews. Furthermore, Jacob's granddaughter, Judith Bernays Heller, stated that toward the end of Jacob's life, he still studied the Talmud and recited many parts of the Passover Seder by heart. Similarly, Rice presents evidence to suggest that the marriage of Jacob Freud to his bride, Amalia, was solemnized by an Orthodox rabbi.

Based on visitors' recollections that Amalia spoke only Yiddish, Rice concludes that Yiddish must have been Freud's first language, though Freud professed ignorance of both that language and Hebrew. Rice further contends that Freud must have received a Hebrew education as part of his standard Gymnasium curriculum. Jacob Freud placed a Hebrew inscription in the family Bible on the occasion of Sigmund's thirty-fifth birthday, and Rice analyzes it in detail, postulating that a father would not have written an indecipherable message to his son.

In addition to the family Bible, an eight-volume Philippson Bible (1858 edition) was recently discovered in Freud's library. It bore the stamp of "Rabbiner Dr. Altmann" and handwritten notes. How the work came into Freud's possession is not clear. What is certain, however, is that the work was previously owned by Rabbi Dr. Adolf (Avraham) Altmann (see Introductory Note to Chapter III), an eminent scholar and historian, who served as rabbi in Salzburg from 1907-1915 and subsequently became Chief Rabbi of Trier, Germany. His sole surviving son, Dr. Manfred Altman of London, confirms that both the stamp and the handwritten notes in question are definitely those of his father.

Freud's denial of Jewish linguistic and religious knowledge is but one indication of his strong inner conflict about his Jewish identity. Publicly, he had no synagogue affiliation, nor did he practice any religious ritual. On the contrary, he was an avowed atheist, who wrote to Oskar Pfister: "Quite by the way, why did none of the devout create psychoanalysis? Why did one have to wait for a completely godless Jew?"

Yet Freud spent his life interpreting dreams, a divinely inspired activity (Genesis 40:8), and alleviating the pain of his neurotic patients. By contrast, many of his contemporaries were verbal theists who constantly were changing the meaning of their gods based on philosophical concepts of the day, all the while never interpreting dreams nor trying to understand or advance the human condition. In such instances, who really believes in the essence of religion -- the professed atheist or the verbal theist?

Rice blames Freud's seeming rebellion against his Jewish origins on two primary, interrelated factors. The first is the fact that the Freuds were outsiders, Austro-Hungarians (Ostjuden), among the Viennese middle class. The intense prejudice against these Eastern European Jews had a profound effect on the self-esteem of these immigrants and their descendants. Freud attempted to eliminate any aspect of his family history that indicated its Eastern European origins. He created a "family romance," stating (in *An Autobiographical Study*): "I have reason to believe that my father's family were settled for a long time on the Rhine (at Cologne)..." We must move beyond an image that the Freud family itself helped to construct. Second, Freud had ambivalent feelings toward his father, Jacob, who had caused him to be an outsider. He felt the death of his father very passionately. Rice sees in this relationship the classic Oedipal father-son conflict, not exclusively in sexual terms, but also in terms of power and authority. Both of these factors could account for the discrepancies between the public persona of Freud and his private, inner self.

The biblical figure of Moses fascinated Freud for almost his entire life. His *Moses and Monotheism* represented a continuation and ultimately, the culmination of his quest for personal identity. In his attempt to write a biography of the Jewish people, Freud succeeded in writing a true autobiography. It is interesting to note that the original title of *Moses and Monotheism* was *The Man Moses: A Historical Novel.* It is possible that the only way Freud, in his old age, could have allowed himself to come to terms with the Judaism of his father was by acting out his own Oedipal complex. In *Moses and Monotheism*, he created a de-Judaized, Egyptian Moses-father, had him murdered by Jews and then created a new, Jewish Moses, with whom he identified.

Freud's extreme identification with Moses led him to appoint Carl Gustav Jung as his "Joshua." He hoped to pass on the leadership of the psychoanalytic movement to a Christian and thereby save it from what he feared would be an irradicable Jewish imprint. Freud wanted psychoanalysis to become a truly universal movement and certainly did not want it to remain a "Jewish science."

Freud's perception (in his preface to the Hebrew edition of *Totem and Taboo*) that he fulfilled the essence of Judaism shows his understanding of the similarity between psychoanalysis and religion. Psychoanalysis ultimately refers to the analysis of the psyche, the essence of the soul and the unconscious. The exploration of the unconscious is an essential aspect of a religious life. Religion is ultimately about the relationship of each individual to humanity and God. While discarding many of his family religious traditions, Freud focused on the essence of the soul and its manifestations.

I would like history to view Freud as "I am Joseph [your brother, the interpreter of dreams]; is my father [Moses] still alive?" (Genesis 45:3)

SELECTED ENGLISH BIBLIOGRAPHY
OF BOOKS DEALING WITH THE RELATIONSHIP OF
JUDAISM AND JUNGIAN PSYCHOLOGY

Cooper, H. (Editor). (1988). *Soul searching: Studies in Judaism and psychotherapy.* London: SCM Press Ltd.

Dreifuss, G. (1984). *Papers: 1965-1984.* Haifa: Private publication.

Edinger, E.F. (1986). *The Bible and the psyche: Individuation symbolism in the Old Testament.* Toronto: Inner City Books.

Jaffe, L.W. (1990). *Liberating the heart: Spirituality and Jungian psychology.* Toronto: Inner City Books.

Kirsch, J. (1973). *The reluctant prophet: An exploration of prophecy and dreams.* Los Angeles: Sherbourne Press, Inc.

Schärf-Kluger, R. (1967). *Satan in the Old Testament.* Translated by Hildegard Nagel. Evanston, Ill.: Northwestern University Press.

Spiegelman, J.M. and Jacobson, A. (Editors). (1986). *A modern Jew in search of a soul.* Arizona: Falcon Press.

Wiener, A. (1978). *The prophet Elijah in the development of Judaism: A depth-psychological study.* London: Routlege and Kegan Paul Ltd.

GLOSSARY OF HEBREW TERMS

Aleph	The first letter of the Hebrew alphabet.
Aron ha-Kodesh	The Holy Ark, found in every synagogue.
Ayin	The 16th letter of the Hebrew alphabet.
Baal Shem Tov	Rabbi Israel ben Eliezer (18th century), founder of Hassidism, a movement that stressed the ordinary person's way of reaching God.
Bar-Mitzvah	The age of maturation (13) for a Jewish male.
Bara	God created.
Bashert	Fate.
Basherte	A predestined spouse.
Bat Kol	A heavenly voice.
Bat-Mitzvah	The age of maturation (12) for a Jewish female.
Bet	The second letter of the Hebrew alphabet.
Boker Tov	Good morning.
Charut	Engraved.
Cherut	Freedom.
Dalet	The fourth letter of the Hebrew alphabet.
Ed	Witness.
Ehad	One.
Gematria	Numerology.

Hakreh	Happening; "coincidence."
Halakhah	Jewish law.
Halakhic	In accordance with Jewish law.
Sefer HaPekudim	The Book of Census and Travels, i.e., Numbers.
Hassidic	An 18th century movement that stressed the ordinary person's way of reaching God.
Hok	A statute, i.e., a Jewish law whose reason has not been revealed.
Ish	"Man." See Chapter VI.
Kabbalah	Jewish mysticism.
Karav	To come close.
Kavvanah	Appropriate intention in the performance of commandments.
Kedushah	Holiness; separateness; numinosity.
Keriah	The rending of a mourner's garment.
Kol Yaakov Hai	The voice of Jacob lives.
Koran Or Panav	His face beamed with light.
Korban	A sacrificial offering.
Maggid	A story-teller.
Mezid	Intentional sin.
Midrash	A homiletical explanation.

Mikdash Me'at	A miniature sanctuary.
Mikreh	Happening; "coincidence."
Minyan	Quorum required for communal prayer.
Mishneh Torah	1) Deuteronomy, the last book of the Torah. 2) A Code of Law by Maimonides.
Mitzvah	A commandment.
Mitzvat Anashim Melumada	The practice of commandments as an intellectual habitual exercise.
Mitzvot	Commandments.
Na'aseh ve-Nishma	Literally, "We will do and we will listen." Figuratively, the Israelites' unqualified acceptance of the Torah.
Nachat	Pride.
Nefesh	Life; soul.
Olam Katan	The concept of each individual as a microcosm.
Pesach	The holiday of Passover.
Rebbe	Personal spiritual mentor.
Rosh Hashanah	The Jewish New Year.
Ru'ah	Breath; wind; spirit.
Ru'ah ha-Kodesh	The holy spirit.
Seder	Literally, "order." A Passover celebration.
Sefer HaGeulah	The Book of Redemption, i.e., Exodus.

Sefer HaKedushah The Book of Holiness, i.e., Leviticus.

Sefer HaYetzira   The Book of Creation, i.e., Genesis.

Shabbat   The Jewish Sabbath.

Shalom Aleikhem "Peace be unto you," a greeting.

Shamoa Tishma   "You will surely hear."

Shavuot   The holiday of Pentecost.

Shekhinah   The Feminine Divine Presence.

Shema Yisroel   Literally, "Hear, O Israel." Figuratively, this refers to the Jewish declaration of faith.

Shoah   The European destruction of Jews carried out by Germany's Third Reich.

Shogeg   Unintentional sin.

Sukkot   The holiday of Tabernacles.

Tehom   Depth.

Teshuvah   Repentance.

Tikkun ha-Olam   The human's continuous maintenance and improvement of God's world.

Tohu va-Vohu   The state of utter void and chaos that existed during the Creation process.

Torah   The Pentateuch.

Torah im Derekh   The integration of religious life with general
  Eretz   knowledge.

Torah u-Mada	The synthesis of Torah and general knowledge.
Tzel	Shadow.
Tzelem	Image.
VaYikra	"And He called." The first word of Leviticus, the third book of the Torah.
Yaakov Avinu Lo Met	"Jacob, our father, has not died."
Yahrzeit	Anniversary of a death.
Yetzer ha-Ra	The capacity to do evil.
Yetzer ha-Tov	The capacity to do good.
Yom Kippur	The Day of Atonement.

NAME INDEX

Note: *"Rabbi" refers to a rabbi who is mentioned in the Talmud.*

SUBJECT INDEX

ABOUT THE AUTHOR

Levi Meier, Ph.D., is Chaplain at Cedars-Sinai Medical Center and a psychologist in private practice in Los Angeles, CA. He received his M.S. in gerontology and Ph.D. in psychology from the University of Southern California. Rabbi Meier was ordained at Yeshiva University, where he received an M.A. in Jewish Philosophy. Through his varied and extensive clinical and educational background, he serves interchangeably as rabbi, psychologist, gerontologist and thanatologist. This is the fourth book in his series on Jewish values. The first three are entitled *Jewish Values in Bioethics, Jewish Values in Psychotherapy* and *Jewish Values in Health and Medicine.* He is also Special Issues Editor of the *Journal of Psychology and Judaism.*